S0-DQW-928

ULTREIA

(Go Farther)

By the same author

FAN THE FLAME

HIGHER THAN I

ULTREIA

Meditations for
Spiritual Direction

ROB DES COTES

IMAGO DEI PUBLISHING

Ultreia
Copyright © 2010 by Rob Des Cotes
All rights reserved.

Image Dei Publishing
19353-16th Avenue
Surrey, BC V3S 9V2 Canada
www.imagodeicommunity.ca

Unless otherwise noted, all Scripture quotations are from the
HOLY BIBLE, NEW INTERNATIONAL VERSION
copyright © 1973, 1978, 1984 by the International Bible Society.

Cover design by Rob Clements and Rob Des Cotes

Library and Archives Canada Cataloguing in Publication

Des Cotes, Rob, 1954-
Ultreia : meditations for spiritual direction / Rob Des Cotes.

Includes bibliographical references.
ISBN 978-0-9920592-1-7

1. Bible—Meditations. 2. Meditation—Christianity.
3. Spiritual life—Christianity. I. Title.

BV4813.D48 2010   248.3'4

CONTENTS

INTRODUCTION

Those who have walked the Camino de Santiago pilgrimage route in the south of France and northern Spain are familiar with a song often heard at hostels or churches along the way. The song is "Ultreia," and the ancient words: "Ultreia, ultreia, e suseia, Deus adjuvanos" roughly translate as, "Go farther, go higher, may God be your help."

It is a song of encouragement to those who still have a distance to go and who might be sensing a weariness settling in their spirits. It offers spiritual direction to those who have lost their way, and motivation to those who have forgotten why they began this path in the first place. For those tempted with discouragement, it gives hope that our destination, though seemingly far away, is nevertheless within reach. And finally it is a song that recognizes that we need God's help if we are to finish well, for our journey can easily be subverted.

Ultreia is ultimately a song of community. It recognizes that we need each other's help if we are to travel farther and higher in this journey. It is a song we sing to one another whenever we notice the discouragement or disorientation that happens to all of us at times. We call out to those who are lagging behind, "press on, press on, we are almost there!"

Such is the spirit of this book and its intent. These meditations are sign-posts along the way that remind us of the path we are invited to respond to in the offering of our lives. They are meant as encouragements for us to go farther and to not stop short of the fullness of Christ that is possible in our lives. In the otherwise solitary journey of the spiritual life, they remind us that we are not alone. We are part of a large and historic community of those "who have set their hearts on pilgrimage" (Ps. 84:5).

The loosely-knit network that we call *Imago Dei* is a catalyst that encourages anyone who longs for fellowship along the journey of conversion to gather with kindred seekers. A variety of resources created for Imago Dei groups, as well as for personal use, can be found on our website (www. imagodeicommunity.ca). You are not alone. Many in the world have sensed the invitation to surrender more fully to Christ's transforming purpose through contemplative prayer. As we respond daily to this gift of faith, may we too sing out to all who walk beside us: "Go farther, go higher. May God be your help."

As always, I am grateful for the wonderfully diverse communities of Imago Dei and for the many spiritual friends who form them. You mirror and affirm my own deepest longings for God and for the spiritual community I know is possible. Blessings to all who long for more. May the Lord give us grace to sustain us in these good desires.

Rob Des Cotes
Loyola House
Guelph, Ontario
May, 2010

MEDITATIONS

1

Small is the gate and narrow the road that leads to life, and only a few find it.

Matthew 7:13-14

I often think of the spiritual life as a funnel, gathering us from far and wide and leading us towards the narrow spout of heaven. As it draws us towards the gates of salvation, the way gets narrower until it leads to the one opening that Christ has provided. It is a helpful image that applies not only to our personal spiritual direction but also as an aid in understanding how God works with people wherever they are in relationship to faith.

At the mouth of the funnel there is a width and breadth to the spiritual life. Religions have much in common with one another here, as do good people of many persuasions. Many truths seem interchangeable. The boundaries, being the circumference of the mouth, have enough definition to indicate a spiritual life, but there is too much latitude for truth to have any real precision. Many people prefer to remain at the mouth of the funnel, never letting themselves be carried deeper towards the spout.

As we move further into the funnel we find the walls narrowing. The boundaries that define truth seem closer to one another as we are being shepherded towards the narrow gate. Things that didn't necessarily apply to us when we were at the mouth of the funnel now become important as we welcome the precision they bring to our bearings. We recognize, in the restrictions of good theology, a source of spiritual vitality. Though the walls are closer now than we first imagined necessary, and though there is less room for movement, the thought of returning to the wider boundaries of the funnel mouth seems counter-productive to the direction we now seek.

As we near the spout, the walls that separate truth from untruth are very close on either side of us. Like paddles that push us back onto the path whenever we stray, the truth now more insistently corrects us from our deviations. The way has become narrow and the passage feels extremely tight as we brush up against correctives at every turn.

As we habituate to the narrowness of the spiritual life, our perception also changes in relationship to what we once considered liberty. In spite of greater restrictions to the soul, we find that we no longer miss the width and breadth of our former illusions of freedom. We sense and are comforted instead by the guiding hands of God on all sides of our life. Like a river that enters the narrow chasm, we feel the strength of spiritual life flow through these hands. We have been led through the funnel, from the weaker life of the wider way, to the narrow life that Jesus calls abundant.

2

In all your ways acknowledge him,
and he will make your paths straight

Proverbs 3:6

Imagine three ships sailing the open seas. They must navigate by getting their bearings "from above"—according to the sun and stars. By projecting themselves to a point other than themselves, they are able to look back, determine their present position, and adjust their course accordingly.

Now imagine if each of these three ships were to check its bearings at different intervals—the first ship every few days, the second one daily, and the third ship every hour. If we were to chart their travels on a map we can well imagine what the three different trajectories would look like.

It is very likely that the path of the first ship, the one that checked its bearings only occasionally, would zig-zag. It would inevitably stray from its course until it eventually corrected itself every few days. Once it had recovered its bearings it would be aimed in the right direction but, before long, it would likely wander again from its course.

The second ship, the one that adjusted its course every day, would naturally be less delinquent. Its calculations would certainly reveal corrections to be made, but likely not as drastic as those needed for the first ship. It is obvious that it would be the third ship, the one that checks in every hour, whose trajectory would show the least wobble. If it did stray, it would only be for a short time before its deviations were noted and corrected.

This illustration is as easy to understand as the Scripture it depicts. If we don't acknowledge God in "all our ways," our path will likely wander and wobble much more than if we checked in more frequently. Could it be any simpler?

3

> The LORD said, "Go out and stand on the mountain in the presence of the LORD, for the LORD is about to pass by."
> Then a great and powerful wind tore the mountains apart and shattered the rocks before the LORD, but the LORD was not in the wind. After the wind there was an earthquake, but the LORD was not in the earthquake. After the earthquake came a fire, but the LORD was not in the fire. And after the fire came a gentle whisper. When Elijah heard it, he pulled his cloak over his face and went out and stood at the mouth of the cave.
>
> 1 Kings 19:11-13

The story of God revealing Himself to Elijah in a gentle whisper reveals something of the way God ministers to us all. Before speaking a word to our lives, the Lord has to first pacify the turmoil that hinders our hearing. He leads us from a state of unrest to a spirit of peace from which we can better receive His presence.

Prior to this passage, Elijah has just had a showdown with the prophets of the Phoenician god, Baal. Winning the contest has resulted in the people turning against the prophets of Baal, killing every one of them. When Jezebel, the Phoenician queen of Israel, hears of this she swears a maledictory oath and sends word to Elijah saying, "So may the gods do to me, and more also, if I do not make your life like the life of one of them by this time tomorrow." She wants Elijah's head, and in a state of panic, he runs away to hide.

God meets him in the desert and asks, "What are you doing here, Elijah?" In desperation Elijah replies, "I have been very zealous for the Lord, the God of hosts; for the Israelites have forsaken your covenant, thrown down your altars, and killed your prophets with the sword. I alone am left, and they are seeking my life, to take it away." The prophet is angry, his soul is in turmoil and he vents his frustration to God. What happens next is curious. Rather than deal with the content of his reply, the Lord instead turns His attention to Elijah's state of soul. He suggests a "time-out" and tells Elijah, "Go out and stand on the mountain before the Lord, for the Lord is about to pass by."

As though mirroring the turmoil in Elijah's soul, God sends a great wind and allows it to be known that He is not in the wind. The wind is followed by an earthquake, and then by fire. These are violent expressions of nature which reflect Elijah's inner spirit. Again, the Lord makes known that He is not to be found in such states of agitation. Then comes a gentle whisper, "the sound of sheer silence." In this last manifestation, Elijah finally recognizes the Spirit of God's presence. Only then does the Lord resume his conversation, repeating the same question as before, "What are you doing here, Elijah?" The person the Lord is now speaking to, however, is not the same as before. He has been transformed into one who is now able to hear.

It is difficult to discern God's voice from an agitated state. Unfortunately, that is the state of soul from which we most acutely feel the need for God. We feel desperate. But, as we are told in Psalm 46, we must first "be still" before we can know the Lord. And this more receptive state is what God leads us to through prayer.

Elijah expected God to meet him in his place of turmoil, but the Lord was not prepared to do so. Instead, He ministered to the prophet's spirit. Before speaking with him about his predicament, God had to first deal

MEDITATIONS FOR SPIRITUAL DIRECTION

with the anxiety that Elijah felt about his situation. The Lord subdued him with a whisper in order to finally speak to him, Spirit to spirit. And so He does with us.

4

Let your gentleness be evident to all. The Lord is near.
Philippians 4:5

The spiritual life, most simply defined, is the art and discipline of remaining present to God. You would think that nothing could be easier for us to do. But in order to remain in the presence of God it is necessary for us to cultivate certain virtues that are congruent with divinity. Foremost among these virtues is that of gentleness.

Gentleness makes us hospitable to God's presence. In his book *Spirituality and the Gentle Life*, Adrian Van Kaam affirms the benefits of cultivating such an inner disposition. He writes,

> Gentleness is an important condition for the spiritual life. The life of the spirit emerges and grows in gentility. A gentle life style affects all my ways. It changes my view of myself and others. It makes me work, speak, feel and act in a different manner. It creates an atmosphere that is truly conducive to worship and surrender.

Gentleness, of course, begins at home. If we are not gentle with ourselves we cannot expect to be gentle with others, nor with God. To be gentle with myself is to welcome all I see inside me as precious, fragile and vulnerable. Van Kaam recognizes that we must approach our fragile self as God does—with compassion and kindness. He writes,

> A first step to inner gentleness is to gratefully love myself as a unique divine gift and to admit and accept the very weakness which makes me the fragile earthen vessel of this treasure. Gentleness with self is possible only when I recognize and "own" the vulnerability of who I am.

To live gently is to live in Divine likeness. Jesus said of Himself, "I am gentle and humble in heart." When I lose my gentleness, I lose a basic point of fellowship with the presence of God. Gentleness then is a pathway to prayer. It is one of the means by which we are to remain in Christ's love (Jn 15:1).

But there are movements within us that oppose this virtue, that thwart the gentleness of our relationship with God. When it comes to the finesse of spirituality I can often feel like the proverbial "bull in a china shop." Van Kaam describes the humble and childlike disposition that gentleness requires of us and the willful spirit that opposes it. He writes,

> Most fragile is my presence to the Divine; only grace can maintain it. Awareness of the Divine is subtle and sublime, of such fragility and finesse that it may disappear the moment my willfulness and pride take over and try to force the felt presence of this Infinite Guest. The divine gift of gentility thus keeps at bay any arrogant movement on my part that might chase away the loving presence of the Holy.

To be gentle is to be hospitable to God's spirit. To maintain this state however requires that we be attentive to the ever-changing ground of our being, and that we recognize early the first signs of its hardening. If we don't catch these changes at the onset they will de-sensitize us to the subtle presence of God. Van Kaam describes his own relationship to gentleness lost, and to its recovery.

> I drop my prayers to gain time for action. I skip moments of rest and recollection. No longer do I find time to gently nurse my soul. I have put myself into captivity. Now is the time to call upon the Lord. He will bring me back from my captivity. He will grace me with gentility. Instead of my tasks captivating me, I shall carry them. He will help me to break their overly busy hold on my life, teaching me how I can maintain myself gently in regard to them. He will help me to still and quiet my soul, to nurse it back to life as gently as a nursing mother.

Gentleness in our lives fosters a more consistent awareness of our relationship with God. It is a virtue to be embraced by all who cherish the spiritual life. Explore for yourself how this Christ-like virtue helps you remain more consistently in God's presence. See what changes you notice in the disposition of your soul as you make gentleness a focus of your prayer. Let it be the grace that you seek from God today.

Take my yoke upon you and learn from me, for I am gentle and humble in heart, and you will find rest for your souls.

Matthew 11:29

5

For their sakes I sanctify myself.

John 17:19 (KJV)

People have long misunderstood the agenda of men and women who withdraw from the active life in order to more earnestly seek God. "What good do they do for the world?" they ask. And yet those who retreat from the active life often do so in response to a profound insight regarding the relationship between their own pursuit of God, and the most pressing spiritual needs of the world. They recognize how cultivating a life of prayer is a direct means of loving the world, and of expediting God's ultimate purposes for it.

As we participate in our own spiritual growth, we inevitably contribute to God's purposes for the world. The sanctification that the Holy Spirit brings about in us individually is directly related to the growth of the whole. In seeking this, we come to love the world as Jesus did, sharing something of the same incentive for spiritual obedience that He expressed when He said: "For their sakes I sanctify myself."

Like the first rays of dawn that eventually fill the whole sky with light, the knowledge and experience of Jesus' presence on earth is increasing daily (Col. 1:6). As each of us more truly reflects the character of God, the Light that shines through humanity does so ever brighter. As first fruits of the kingdom (James 1:18) we are to become the very change that we know God wants to see in the world.

For their sakes I sanctify myself. The most we can do for one another is to seek and find God in our lives. As we are transformed in this process, we will more fully reflect, so that others might more clearly see, the light of Truth in the world. The Day will soon come when each of our lives will fully reflect this Light. May we hasten that Day as we see it approaching and, for the sake of those around us, may we seek, in our own lives, its increase.

> *The creation waits in eager expectation for the sons and daughters of God to be revealed.*
>
> Romans 9:19

6

> *It is the glory of God to conceal a matter; to search out a matter is the glory of kings (and queens).*
>
> Proverbs 25:2

We were created in order to seek God's face. This is the very reason we have been given life. As the book of Acts tell us, we were born "so that we would seek God and perhaps reach out for Him and find Him, though He is not far from each one of us" (Acts 17:27). Often and unequivocally, Scripture assures us that if we seek the Lord, we will surely come to find Him. If it is to God's glory to have concealed such a "matter" within the scope of our lives, the book of Proverbs tells us that it is to our own glory to search it out.

In his seminal book on prayer, *The Pursuit of God*, A.W. Tozer describes the spiritual direction that the act of seeking God represents. Tozer sees it as the catalyst for all other spiritual movement. God has placed, deep within our hearts, the invitation to seek His face. Our reflected glory is expressed according to the many ways we respond to that call. Tozer writes,

> He moves us to return. This first comes to our notice when our restless hearts feel a yearning for the Presence of God and we say within ourselves, "I will arise and go to my Father."

The intentional action of the soul's "arising" and "returning," represents the first dynamic motion of the spiritual life. By responding to God's call, we stir a movement in the heart that ultimately defines our spiritual growth and direction. In so doing, we become more fully who God would have us be. As Tozer puts it,

> God wills that we should push on into His Presence and live our whole life there. This is to be known to us in conscious experience. It is more than a doctrine to be held, it is a life to be enjoyed every moment of every day.

The act of pursuing God reciprocally fans the flame of our spiritual desires. Ultimately, this flame will lead us to what our hearts desire most—unity with God. But the experience of finding God does not necessarily satisfy our hunger. It actually quickens our desire for more. Tozer describes the soul's continual outreach for God.

> The moment the Spirit quickens us, our whole being senses its kinship to God and leaps up in joyous recognition. That is the heavenly birth without which we cannot see the Kingdom of God. It is, however, not an end but an inception, for now begins the glorious pursuit, the heart's happy exploration of the infinite riches of the Godhead

To have found God and yet to still pursue Him is the paradox of love. Like the seraphim who are eternally approaching God's light, we are most fully alive when we live in response to our heart's desire for intimacy with God. Blessed are those who devote themselves to seeking the glory that God has hidden within their hearts.

Tozer sums up, in a prayer, the longings that such a pursuit articulates. Perhaps, in his words, we too might find our own deepest desires expressed.

> *O God, I have tasted your goodness, and it has both satisfied me and made me thirsty for more. I am conscious of my need of further grace. I confess my lack of desire O God. I want to want You more; I long to be filled with longing; I thirst to be made more thirsty still. Show me your glory I pray so that I may truly know you.*
>
> — A.W. Tozer

7

Surely you desire truth in the inner parts;
you teach me wisdom in the inmost place.

Psalm 51:6

We are all pretty *ec-centric*. That is, we operate mostly from a position other than the center of our lives. Everything we desire or worry about in this life draws us outwards, towards the periphery of who we are. Countering this, we hear the voice of many Christian saints calling us to return to our center—to the place of our deepest interiority. Their teachings encourage us to draw in from the outer edges of our lives in order to live more consistently from a deeper hub.

The spiritual life invites us to change the locus of our being from the surface to the inmost part of our selves. The 17th century mystic, Jeanne Guyon saw this recovery of our center as the natural inclination of our souls. She wrote,

> Inside your spirit there is an act going on. It is a sweet sinking into Deity. The inward attraction—the magnetic pull—becomes more and more powerful. Your soul, dwelling in love, is drawn by this powerful attraction and sinks continually deeper into that love.

Because it is a natural inclination of the soul, one of the ways we most readily "descend" towards the center of our lives is by simply loosening our grip on those things that keep us more attached to the surface. In other words, we move more readily towards the center by letting go of the periphery. Again Guyon writes,

> Nothing is as quick to return to its center as is the soul to the Spirit. Therefore hold your soul at peace. The more peaceful your soul is, the more quickly it is able to move toward God, its center.

Our spiritual disciples, especially the practice of contemplative prayer, encourage a greater capacity for interiority. In time, we learn how to operate more consistently from a deeper place within ourselves. As our capacity for prayer increases we find that it excavates (lit. *hollows out*) a space for God within us. It creates a prayer closet, a back room as it were, to our lives. And, from this place of deeper interiority, we come to understand and to experience more fully the "wisdom in the inmost place" that God most desires for us.

Prayer enlarges the heart until it is capable of containing the gift of God Himself.

— Mother Teresa

8

Now to him who is able to do immeasurably more than all we ask or imagine, according to his power that is at work within us, to him be glory in the church and in Christ Jesus throughout all generations, for ever and ever! Amen.

Ephesians 3:20-21

Scripture encourages us to think in terms of a big God. Whenever we fail to keep this in Biblical perspective all other matters of our faith are diminished. When our God is too small we too suffer from smallness. We become a different kind of Christian, a different type of church—one with a much more diminished sense of itself.

When we no longer expect much from God, we automatically assume that more depends on us. We fall into the illusion that everything— whether prayer, mission or ministry—rises or falls according to our own initiative, or lack thereof. We presume that it is our responsibility to create and manage the church, to save the world, and to bear the fruit of a good Christian life. And, in the end, because our God was too small, we are discouraged.

As we look to ourselves for the measure of spiritual possibility we inevitably end up lowering the bar. Our vision becomes human-sized, and what we expect from ourselves—the fruit of our lives and the influence we could have on the world—is reduced to something much more "realistic" and manageable. Since we don't anticipate much beyond our own capabilities or means, we focus instead on those things that we *can* do for ourselves—programs we could well manage if God weren't around to help us.

But Scripture introduces us to a God who, in every way, surpasses our imagination—a God whose strength and power are surpassingly more than we could ever imagine or conceive of. The truth of the matter is that our God, far from being small, is much too big to fit into our imaginations. If we want to keep to this Biblical perspective, we will need to stop measuring our expectations of what God can do according to the limits of what we conceive possible.

9

There is a time for everything.... a time to tear down and a time to build.

Ecclesiastes 3:1, 3

A regular practice of prayer will inevitably lead us through many terrains of experience. As we return each day to the familiarity of prayer we will come to know the subtle changes that take place in the spiritual environment. We will become familiar with the spiritual landscape in ways that we never could if we only prayed sporadically.

The atmosphere of prayer is always fluctuating. From solid to fluid, from opaque to transparent, from thick to thin, there is a wide spectrum of metaphors that can be used to describe our varying sense of it. Our experiences can range from an overwhelming sense of relationship to one of complete isolation. They can lead to times of deep satisfaction or to times of desperation with regards to our hopes for divine relationship. As we become more and more familiar with these varied expressions, we also find that different states of soul will, at times, necessitate different approaches to prayer.

Because of the very changeability it highlights, we are encouraged by the Holy Spirit to experiment in our approaches to prayer. At times we will be invited to explore freedom—to break down rigid patterns or methods that we've been relying on in order to simply let ourselves "float" in the experience of prayer-in-the-moment. For days or weeks, this type of exploration might be the prime objective of our prayer time. It is a "time to tear down" and, for a season, this approach might provide us with the greatest sense of truth in our relationship with God.

It is inevitable though that, sooner or later, such an amorphous approach will no longer yield the same sense of truth as it once did. It will start to feel more and more aimless, without strength of purpose. The time has likely come to exercise a more disciplined approach to prayer. We will know that it is now a "time to build up." In this season, a more structured tact will surely bear the best fruit. Formal prayers, the use of the imagination, or of a centering mantra might now provide the best foundation from which to rebuild the integrity of our prayer relationship.

Prayer defies our attempts to predict or control its outcome, and the Holy Spirit will indicate, usually through our sense of dissatisfaction, when it is time to move from one approach to another. As the Holy Spirit breaks the fallow ground of familiarity, we should always anticipate that a method that seemed to work yesterday might well have to be abandoned tomorrow.

10

Unless you change....you will never enter the kingdom of heaven.
Matthew 18:3

My wife and I recently returned from our third leg of walking the Camino de Santiago, a 12th-century pilgrimage route that starts in France and ends, some 1500km later, in Santiago, Spain. We first began exploring this path six years ago with a short week-long excursion of 165km. We were so taken by the experience that it has completely redefined our notion of holidays. Besides the beautiful landscapes and the rich fare of people, food and culture, one of the important things we feel called to continue exploring is the inner transformation that takes place over time as we simplify our lives, becoming more focused, more integrated in body, mind and soul. After our initial foray of one week it was obvious to ask ourselves, "How much deeper would this transformation go if we gave it more time?"

We have since returned twice more to continue other legs of this pilgrimage, each time for a longer duration. We envy those who are able to take three months to walk the entire 1500km in one journey. But, in our incremental way, we are learning much about the changes that take place within us as we allow more time for the spiritual life to deepen. I mention all this because a similar deepening has taken place over the years in my prayer life that I recognize is also related to the amount of time I allot to it.

Much of what happens in our extended prayer has to do with the subtle transformation we undergo as we sit quietly before God. A gradual settling and focusing take place that only time and patience can produce. It requires faith in order to believe that such a state of rest lies beyond the initial turmoil that often defines the onset of our prayer time. And it takes patience to remain in place long enough to experience it.

Often it is only in the final few minutes of prayer that we finally approach the state of soul we have been seeking. And this, only if we haven't given up on the process beforehand. Before we get to God, it would seem that we have to first get over ourselves. We have to pass through the desert of self before we reach the oasis of prayer that we seek. This is the hard work of prayer. As Richard Rohr observes, "That is why the first twenty minutes are usually so tedious. For the first twenty minutes only the primary agenda shows itself." Of course it shouldn't surprise us that it takes time for the spirit of peace to establish itself in our hearts. Prayer, after all, is quite a different state of soul than the active one from which we first set out.

By simply extending the duration of our prayer time, new possibilities for relationship with God and with ourselves are created. In my own experience, a longer prayer time has allowed me to be more patient with myself in terms of the process of transformation. I am no longer anxious about time wasted by my rambling thoughts as I accept that as a natural part of the preliminary stage of prayer. I am prepared to let myself be more gradually subdued by peace.

We can't force nor rush the process by which we open up to God. Transformation takes time. But we can create more space in our lives in order for this work to unfold. The experience of many is that, by simply offering time to God, the Holy Spirit mysteriously leads us, along the path of spiritual transformation, to that which our hearts seek.

11

*When Elizabeth heard Mary's greeting, the baby leaped in her
womb, and Elizabeth was filled with the Holy Spirit.*

Luke 1:41

It happens at various points in our spiritual life that seeds are planted
within us in the form of a profound experience of God. It might be an
experience of being particularly loved by God, or perhaps a deep peace
that settles the soul. Or maybe it is a joy, somehow related to eternity, that
fills our heart with new longings. Such epiphanies have the power to reset
our lives. They change the course of our spiritual direction from one of
searching for "I know not what," to a more deliberate quest to return to
"that which I have once tasted of God."

Such seems to have been the case with John the Baptist. While still in
his mother Elizabeth's womb, John experienced a profound recognition of
Christ which thereafter set the course for his adult life. In response to the
sound of Mary's greeting, Elizabeth exclaimed that the baby within her
leapt for joy. This encounter precipitated an experience, for both mother
and unborn child, of being filled with the Holy Spirit.

In recognizing the presence of Jesus, a Divine seed was planted in
John's heart. Such a pre-natal memory likely determined the course of
his future life and ministry—his destiny to search for the Messiah he had
once met while still in his mother's womb. It was given to this greatest of
prophets to recognize and identify, in the flesh, that which he had already
known in his spirit

We have no records of Jesus and John the Baptist having any contact
with each other in their upbringing. Though distantly related, John did
not know Jesus by sight when he first met his Lord at the Jordan river. But
though he did not know the face of the Messiah he was seeking, John was
confident that he would recognize Christ when he encountered Him. His
own heart would once again leap for joy, as it did over thirty years ago, at
the Divine Presence, manifest in Jesus.

As God graces our own lives with spiritual experiences, we naturally
seek to return to such places. Having tasted something of the Lord's
presence we now know how near such an encounter is to our lives. These

fleeting experiences serve to authenticate what we believe is possible in the spiritual life. As a foretaste of the relationship that our hearts are meant to enjoy forever, they intensify our desires for God through the tangible memories they produce in us. No longer is our spiritual hope a matter of wishful thinking. We have tasted something of God and it has birthed in us a yearning to return to the Source of what remains so delectable in the soul's memory.

John the Baptist spent the rest of his life searching for the familiar knowledge of Christ that he once experienced in the womb. Perhaps the Lord has implanted such similar memories in our souls as well. As we recognize the signs of Christ in our lives, it is no wonder this is often experienced as something already familiar—as though God has hidden an experience of Himself deep in our soul's memory, knowing that, sooner or later, we will recognize it when we meet Him again.

> *You breathed fragrance, and I drew in my breath, and I now pant for you; I tasted and now I hunger and thirst; you touched me and now I burn for Your peace.*
>
> —Augustine, *Confessions*

12

> *When you are on your beds,*
> *search your hearts and be silent.*
>
> Psalm 4:4

Silence is God's first language. It precedes creation. It is the wellspring from which all life, including the very utterance of our own lives, is drawn. And our returning there pays homage to this fact. As the French philosopher Max Picard says in his book, *The Word of Silence,*

> Silence is the central place of faith where we give the Word back to God from whom we first received it. Surrendering the Word, we surrender the medium of our creation. We "unsay" ourselves, voluntarily returning to the source of our being where we must trust God to "say" us once again.

Barbara Brown Taylor, in her book, *When God Is Silent,* similarly writes,

> In silence, we travel back in time to the day *before* the first day of creation, when all being was still in God. It had not yet been said, and silence was the womb in which it slept.

Contemplative prayer, as it seeks such primordial silence, must first quell the many other dialogues that act as bridges in our relationship with God, and with ourselves. As useful as these are at certain points in our spiritual formation, as we mature, we are invited to let go of these constructions in favour of a more immediate relationship with the Truth. It is only after we stop uttering God that God can freely declare Himself to us. And it is only once we stop uttering our selves, that we discover who we essentially are.

We carry run-on dialogues with ourselves because we are deathly afraid of non-being. As long as chatter is going on in some form within us we are assured of our existence. Resting in silence, however, requires faith that we exist apart from our own self-begetting. It trusts the fact that our existence doesn't depend on our continually creating and re-creating ourselves. By silencing our own self-creation we come to recognize that the life we live is not our own, and that it is Christ, in fact, who lives in us.

The Lord has placed silence as a veil over the threshold of our deepest encounters with the Divine. As countless mystics have experienced, words are no longer necessary once we enter God's presence. In the intimacy of spirit to Spirit communion, they only serve to distance us from the radical immanence of God, who is nearer to us than the word on our lips.

Taylor suggests that, through silence, God protects Himself from the distortions our words otherwise project unto Him.

> Silence becomes God's final defense against our idolatry. By limiting our speech, God gets some relief from our descriptive assaults. By hiding inside a veil of glory, God eludes our projections. God deflects our attempts at control by withdrawing into silence, knowing that nothing gets to us like the failure of our own speech. When we run out of words, then, and perhaps only then, can God be God.

Silence precedes all thought, dogma or pre-conceptions. In embracing its uncreated state we willfully "unsay" ourselves, depending solely on God's word to "say" us once again. The very poverty we experience in silence is an invitation to now receive the truth of who we are and who God is, not as we describe them, but as they are revealed to us.

It is impossible for muddy water to grow clear if it is constantly stirred up.

St. Nilus of Ancrya

13

They that wait upon the LORD shall renew their strength.

Isaiah 40:31 (KJV)

Years of watching my sons play soccer have impressed on me the importance of a key part of a game's strategy as I've often heard a wise coach calling out from the sidelines, "Settle the play." Things get pretty frenetic in competitive sports. Successes go to the head, disappointments deflate the heart, teamwork falls apart and confusion reigns. For the coach to recognize that his team has become unsettled, and to know that dealing with this has to be his first priority, is what makes the difference between recovering your poise or continuing to stumble in the chaos.

The call to "settle the play" is also one that we sense the Holy Spirit shouting to us from the sidelines of our lives. We too get frenetic in our day. Disappointments or troubling thoughts accumulate in us and affect our inner poise. Or maybe it's our sense of teamwork, or our relationships that become confused. We no longer see ourselves as part of a community but somehow start playing as though we were alone on the field. Perhaps it's our successes that have puffed us up, or our mistakes that have shaken our confidence. There isn't time to process all the inner fluctuations that take place in us while the game is on, but their effects nevertheless accumulate. In all these straits the Holy Spirit calls out to us from the sidelines to "settle the play." And by simply taking 5 or 10 minutes to stop and do nothing, we can respond to this call as often as needed.

Taking short pit stops throughout our day gives us time to "dial down" and regroup with God. This is especially needed when we feel the pace of life is becoming unmanageable. Some Benedictine monks have it as a regular discipline in their day to stop for five minutes of prayerful reflection in between each task they complete. Rather than chain-linking all their chores, they stop after one task is finished in order to catch up with themselves. They can then begin the next leg of their day with a fresh spirit.

There is wisdom to the discipline of returning to ourselves often in the course of a day. It is what our spiritual forebears called the "recollection of the soul." The root of the word "recollect" perhaps best expresses the sense of this wisdom. Its Latin etymology means to "gather again in order to remind oneself of something temporarily forgotten." With regards to the spiritual life, it's simply a matter of taking time-outs throughout our day to "settle the play," in order to remember the presence of God in our soul.

14

*Why, O LORD, do you make us wander from your ways
and harden our hearts so we do not revere you?*
                                                    Isaiah 63:17

Sometimes I see things clearly, but often I am blind. Sometimes I am free within myself, but often I feel trapped and constricted. Sometimes I feel very "found" by God, but often I am hopelessly lost. Sometimes I am caught up in the positive momentum of spiritual direction, but often I feel stuck and unproductive.

Such, I am assured, is the common experience of our spiritual lives. I used to believe that I would someday grow out of such states of fluctuating experience—that my times of wandering would be replaced by a more continual sense of being found by God. But that has not been the case. Though such a statement should naturally produce despair in me, I find that it has formed just the opposite—a deeper appreciation that my spiritual life takes place within the mysterious grace of God's initiative of salvation.

These days, I find it easier to accept that there is even some mysterious value in my wandering. If nothing else, it has fashioned and refined the pearl of my longing. Because of the recurring hardness of my heart I treasure even more those rare moments of spiritual sensitivity that grace me at times. Because of the fog that often results from feeling hopelessly lost, the lucid peace of being found again is such a precious experience.

Whereas I once felt apologetic or guilty about my waywardness I now accept this as my starting point. No longer do I see my spiritual stumbling as a matter of falling short of an ideal but rather as the place where, if not for God's grace, I would have no other choice but to be. Where I used to feel afraid and at risk about being lost, I now trust God to not only find me but to continue walking with me in and through my wanderings.

It is easier these days for me to accept that, like most of us, I often fail to live up to my vision of the spiritual life. But it is precisely because of these defeats, and not in spite of them, that I am learning to rest in the sufficiency of God's grace. If nothing else, they teach me patience—how to wait in hope for my Redeemer's initiative. And through the repeated experience of being lost and found, it is becoming easier to believe that God orchestrates even the deficiencies of my heart in order to manifest His over-riding glory

All the days of my hard service, I will wait for my renewal to come.

Job 14:14

15

In this world you will have trouble. But take heart! I have overcome the world.

John 16:33

There is a poignant scene in John Steinbeck's *Grapes of Wrath* where a dust storm has ravaged the corn crop that the farm-tenants depend on for their livelihood. Oklahoma in the 1930s was a time when women and children's survival very much depended on the strength and resilience of their men. Steinbeck describes how the resolve of those men brought hope and assurance to the community around them. In a beautiful study of human empathy the author depicts the women and children as they carefully watch how the men respond to this new crisis.

> Men stood by their fences and looked at the ruined corn, drying fast now, only a little green showing through the film of dust. The men were silent and they did not move often. And the women came out of the houses to stand beside their men—to feel whether this time the men would break. The women studied the men's faces secretly, for the corn could go, as long as something else remained.

The women and children studied the faces of the men in order to determine their own security. In a similar way we derive our confidence by studying Jesus. As part of the *Ignatian Spiritual Exercises* we are invited to meditate on Jesus' passion and death. We empathize with the anguish of our Lord's suffering as we experience something of the love that compels Him to persevere in this. At His death, like the disciples, we too feel the sense of defeat that threatens all our hopes. But this all changes as we witness Jesus' composure at His resurrection. Steinbeck too describes the power of composure to inspire strength in the midst of apparent defeat.

> After a while, the faces of the watching men lost their bemused perplexity and became hard and angry and resistant. Then the women knew that they were safe and that there was no break. Then they asked, "what'll we do?" and the men replied, "I don't know." But it was all right. Women and children knew deep in themselves that no misfortune was too great to bear if their men were whole.

Through contemplating Christ in His resurrection we share the Lord's satisfaction over the victory that has been established. There is great reassurance in the fulfillment of Christ's words, "I have overcome," that now serves to strengthen us in all our doubts. Our confidence now comes from His confidence.

Christ's death and resurrection have secured us for eternity and, if we should ever doubt this, we need only recall Jesus' words at His post-resurrection appearances and recognize the calm assurances He gives us. "All authority has been given to me....Do not be afraid," the Lord tells us.

In observing Jesus' confidence we are assured that there is truly nothing to fear in this life. He did not break and, like the women and children in Steinbeck's novel, we know deep in our hearts that no misfortune is too great to bear if Jesus stands confident of the final outcome.

16

How great is the love the Father has lavished on us, that we should be called children of God!

1 John 4:1

The apostle John invites us to celebrate the fact that we are now children of God. At 80-something years old, over six decades since he first experienced this new birth for himself, the disciple still marvels at the awesome fact of being called a child of God. But what exactly does John mean by this phrase? Aren't we all "children of God?" Didn't the Jewish Christians he was writing to already assume as much for themselves? Didn't the Greeks also speak in such terms? Doesn't the mere fact of being human mean that we are already children of God?

Christianity makes a radical claim with regards to the potential of human life—that it is possible for human beings to experience a subsequent birth following the inaugural one we all share. Christians, by definition, are those unique people on earth who have begun the process of this second birth. This, and nothing else, is what defines us as children of God. As Paul wrote to the Christians in Rome, only "those who are led by the Spirit of God are the sons and daughters of God" (Rom. 8:14). But the longer you've been a Christian the more likely it is that this truth eludes you. Those who have been Christians their whole lives might not even know what John is talking about here since they've never known any other state. And yet those who are recent converts are likely the ones who marvel most at this radical event that has happened to them.

The gospel plainly states that a literal second birth is possible to all who receive Christ—that there exists the potential of a supernatural birth subsequent to our natural birth. In the prologue to his gospel, speaking of Christ, John writes, "To all who received him, to those who believed in his name, he gave the right to become children of God" (Jn. 1:12). The fact that we have been given the right to now *become* children of God clearly implies that we weren't always so.

John goes on in his prologue to clarify this phrase, defining it as "children born not of natural descent, nor of human decision, but born of God" (Jn. 1:13). Jesus puts it even more plainly when He says, "Flesh gives birth to flesh, but the Spirit gives birth to spirit" (John 3:6). This, John claims, is what makes us children of God—that following our first birth "from below" we now find ourselves, by the grace of Christ, being born "from above" according to the direct initiative of God's Spirit within us. A child of God then, by definition, is one who is God-begotten rather than merely born of the flesh. He/she is a new creation with a new nature that can only come from God's creative seed. That is why Paul is so absolute when he says to the Corinthians, "If anyone is in Christ, he/she is a new creation; the old has gone, the new has come!" (2 Cor. 5:17).

The "second birth" the Scriptures speak of is a literal one. Those who are born from above now have within them a different "seed" than the one they were first born with. They have a different origin which now dictates a different destiny for them. Because of this second birth they are not only different from what they once were but are also different from those around them who cannot imagine such a possibility in life. That is why John tells his hearers that "the reason the world does not know us is that it did not know him" (1 Jn 1:1).

Such is the radical claim of Christianity. Our faith is not primarily a religion. It does not merely offer a different belief system or a different worldview but it testifies to a supernaturally different experience of life that is possible at the core of what it means to be human. Only those who have received Christ can ever truly experience for themselves what this new life represents. Through the ongoing forgiveness of sins and the regeneration of the Holy Spirit they have been given the opportunity to now become "children of God."

17

Let us not give up meeting together, as some are in the habit of
doing, but let us encourage one another—and all the more as
you see the Day approaching.

Hebrews 10:25

Though the original context of this verse is meant to encourage consistency in our fellowship with one another, the same exhortation can also apply to our "meetings" with God. Every saint struggles at times with devotion to prayer. The honest disclosures of the desert hermit Carlo Carretto help identify elements that are common to anyone who endeavours to "not give up meeting together" with God. Carretto speaks frankly about some of the initial hurdles that must be overcome before we reach what the poet Gerard Manley Hopkins calls that "dearest freshness deep down things." Carretto writes,

> You have to break through a certain element of coldness in the first encounter with prayer. Sometimes I have to go for half an hour, or even an hour before making contact with my inner self, before entering into my prayer in any real sense. I too have learned what it means to wrestle with the Angel, as Jacob did that night at the ford. I have learned to appreciate how necessary purification is for our prayer, and that we should not be discouraged by our early difficulties. But I have also learned to savour what follows after the initial coldness, to recognize the first signs of the peace of God, to experience the presence of God and rejoice in his revelation.

There is no magic key that opens the door to intimacy in prayer. No one can "achieve" contemplative prayer. The most we can do is to present ourselves as an offering—to put ourselves in a place where God might grace us with what St. John of the Cross calls "a loving infusion of His presence." Exactly how, when and why this might happen is all up to God. Carretto confers,

> There is no predictable limit set on the delights of prayer, just as there is no limit set on its dryness. The action is always in the hands of God. He is God and I am His creature; He knows and I

do not. It is only right that He should sometimes stand in the way of my haste, or change some plan that I had concocted myself. He, not I, must lay down terms for the dialogue. In the darkest night He is the one who can see the path along which to lead me. Meanwhile, the one thing that gives me strength to pray, or at least to want to pray, is the peace it brings.

From his experience of living for ten years in the desert as one of the Little Brothers of Foucauld, Carretto knows both the struggles as well as the rewards of pursuing God through silent prayer. He encourages anyone who is tempted with discouragement to not give up, for your reward is near.

The resistance you put up to boredom, to distractions and the life around you, your efforts to control your feelings, your imagination, and above all your desire to find God, will slowly but surely bring you into a state of true peace, a peace that is different, not of this world. And then you will begin to acquire a taste for the reality which is forming in the deepest centre of your being; you will learn how better to recognize the least signs of its presence and to sense its unique value.

The writer of Hebrews tells us to "not give up meeting together, as some are in the habit of doing." As we do meet together for fellowship, let us also continue to encourage one another to apply this Scripture to our consistency in meeting with God—and all the more as we see the Day approaching.

18

Where do you think all these appalling wars and quarrels come from? Do you think they just happen? Think again. They come about because you want your own way, and fight for it deep inside yourselves.

James 4:1 (The Message)

It is characteristic of the self-acting soul to be plagued with inner turmoil and strife. For some, the agitations of the heart and mind often become self-destructive as despair and despondency grip the soul.

How does God deal with us in such times? How does the Lord go about subduing the soul that suffers at its own hand?

In Nicholas Evan's novel, *The Horse Whisperer*, Tom Booker is hired to minister his therapy to a prize horse who has suffered a traumatic experience. A truck accident has scarred the horse psychologically, turning it into a violent, angry animal that can no longer be approached. A "horse whisperer" is a trainer who can instinctively understand the motives, needs, and desires of a horse. And this ministry of attentive grace is what is brought to bear in the healing of this animal's psyche.

The first time Tom enters the corral where the horse is kept it responds aggressively to his presence. The therapy has begun and the horse whisperer allows the horse to have its tantrum even at the risk of injuring itself. He then leaves the pen only to return the next day. Once again the horse is allowed to vent her frustrations. After several days of Tom repeatedly establishing his presence in the corral, the horse eventually resigns itself to the fact of his being there.

As Tom now tries to advance and approach the horse, the same violence repeats itself. The horse bucks and charges as it senses its space being encroached. Tom continues to assert his presence and the horse is forced to accept that he is not going to go away and, once again, she settles down.

This process of resistance followed by resignation is repeated at each increasing stage of intimacy until, eventually, Tom is able to stand near the horse, whispering assurances in her ear as he strokes the horse's mane. Through his gentle ministry, the horse whisperer is able to subdue the animal's fears and to pacify it to the point where it can once again be saddled and ridden by its owner.

We too react similarly to the advances of God's intimacy. And we suffer as well from traumas that cause us to react violently at times to the frustrations we feel with ourselves and with the life we live. God understands our fears and the deep-seated reasons we buck at Him, at others, or at ourselves. The Lord longs to minister His peace to us, but this too is something that we resist.

It is natural that the self-willed soul should rail at the suggestion of submission that the spiritual life implies. We buck at the thought of wearing God's saddle. But like the horse whisperer, Jesus is already with us in the corral and He is not going away. We can rant and rave all we want but He will not leave us until He has brought us to a place of inner healing. In the meantime we listen for the voice of the Holy Spirit who continually whispers assurances in our ears. "Surrender to God," we hear Him say to us. Eventually, we give up the fight and allow ourselves to come more fully under the reins of God.

The mind controlled by the Spirit is life and peace.

Romans 8:6

19

Therefore let us leave the elementary teachings about Christ and go on to maturity.

Hebrews 6:1

In chapters 5 and 6 of the book of Hebrews we are warned against the very real possibility of losing momentum in our faith pilgrimage. The writer cautions those who are unwilling to deepen their faith that the full implications of Christ's work will never be grasped nor fully applied to their lives if they do not strive to continually grow. He goes so far as to suggest that ongoing resistance to spiritual growth may even lead us to fall away from God as we harden our hearts against His purposes in us.

The Jewish believers, to whom this book was written, had been Christians for a number of years and the writer exhorts them to show the same diligence in desiring and pursuing growth in the Lord as they had in the beginning. Having reached a certain level of maturity, some now seem to be uninterested or unwilling to press on further. In Hebrews 5:11-12 he rebukes them saying

> We have much to say about this, but it is hard to explain because you are slow to learn. In fact, though by this time you ought to be teachers, you are looking for someone to teach you the elementary truths of God's word all over again.

The phrase, "slow to learn," can be literally translated as, "dull with respect to what is heard." Despite their initial enthusiasm as Christians, a sluggishness has crept in and the writer fears that they have lost interest in growing any further in their faith. One of the signs of their arrested development is their unwillingness or inability to teach others. It seems that they are content to hear over and over again the same reassurances of the elementary truths of faith they have heard from the beginning. By now they should not only be well-acquainted with this basic knowledge but should be more than able to teach it to others while, at the same time, desiring more solid food for themselves. What the writer is identifying here is a serious state of arrested spiritual growth. And his caution is one that Christians at every stage of maturity should heed.

Athletes or musicians know that in order to continue growing in their disciplines they must continually present themselves with new challenges. Once they have reached a certain level of achievement, whether at the bench press or at the metronome, they must then raise the bar if they are to grow beyond their present capacity. To simply keep repeating their previous accomplishments would be a sure way to stunt their development.

Spiritual progress is not something that is achieved by repeatedly "laying the foundation." We grow rather by building *upon* the foundation that has been laid. If we are not continually seeking and finding a "meatier" diet for ourselves, our growth will be stunted like that of a malnourished child.

Once we have incorporated the "elementary teachings of the faith" we must build the mysterious particularity of our spiritual life upon this foundation. It is a time to diligently seek the Holy Spirit in prayer, asking, "What does it mean for me to continue growing as a spiritual man or woman?" "What does the next level of maturity look like for me?" "How can I build upon the foundation that You have already laid in me?" In response to such earnest prayers the Lord will lead us to the deeper, meatier truths that will feed our hungry spirits. He will adjust our diets according to our increasing capacity for solid foods.

20

Blessed are they who hunger and thirst...

Matthew 5:6

When a baby loses its appetite it is natural for the mother to be concerned about what is ailing her child. Conversely, it brings the mother great satisfaction to see her baby eating well as this is a sign that heralds health and growth. Our appetite for the spiritual life is also something that comes and goes, and it is easy to imagine our heavenly Father experiencing the same concern or satisfaction regarding our hunger that a mother would for her baby.

To lose our appetite for God is a sign of illness. Something is wrong in our spiritual system. We have lost our vitality and we need to be nursed back to health. Simple rest is often the best medicine. That is why retreats are so beneficial for helping us recover our appetites for God. An overactive life often becomes an excuse for skimping on lunch, or forgetting to eat altogether. It also has much the same effect in suppressing our spiritual appetite. So does a poor diet. When our teenage son, who usually has a hearty appetite, doesn't feel like finishing his supper it is probably because he has been snacking on junk food. Instead of directing his hunger towards the substantial meal that was waiting for him at home, he has placated it instead with short-term carbohydrates that now leave him with little incentive to eat.

When it comes to spirituality, hunger is a sign of health and vitality. To lose our appetite for God is a sickness, ultimately a sickness unto death. And to treat ourselves as ailing whenever we lose our desire for the spiritual life might be the first step towards the recovery of our vital signs.

21

Jesus Christ, who gave himself for us to redeem us from all wickedness and to purify for himself a people that are his very own, eager to do what is good.

Titus 2:1

Teresa of Avila once pictured the Holy Spirit in the form of water being directed, through prayer, towards the "garden" of our lives. The purpose of such divine irrigation is that flowers of virtue may grow within us. For Teresa, prayer was never an end in itself. It was always a means to righteousness and purity of heart. No matter how beautiful and moving our experience of God in prayer may be, it must always be suspect if it does not also lead to virtue in our lives. Paul, in this verse from his letter to Titus, implies that the cultivation of such righteousness is the very purpose for which Christ has claimed us.

E.M. Bounds, a 19th century American pastor who preached extensively on prayer, says much the same when he writes, "The very end and purpose of the atoning work of Christ is to create religious character and Christian conduct." Bounds stresses that prayer is the most direct means to this end, "Prayer," he teaches, "promotes righteous living, and is the one great aid to uprightness of heart and life."

As prayer invites the Holy Spirit to fashion us according to God's will, it becomes a daily catalyst for the transformation of our character and conduct. The love that we express for God in this relationship of prayer directly influences our behaviour as it encourages our personalities to do and become whatever is most pleasing to the Lord.

Through prayer, sensitivity and remorse for sin become heightened. This increased awareness of the critical need for change at the core of our being can often make us feel hypocritical in our piety. But perseverance in prayer ultimately produces its good fruit by drawing out from within us all that is inordinate and raising it up to the altar of change. Through the gradual exchange of the old for the new we witness the miracle of Christ's righteousness being imparted to us. If we are people of prayer the eventuality of this outcome is inevitable. As E.M. Bounds observed, "Prayer and sinning cannot keep company with each other. One or the other must necessarily stop."

Prayer cultivates a tender disposition that recoils from all that is wrong within us. At the same time it increases our desire to love whatever is most pleasing to our Lord. By placing our lives each day upon the altar of transformation we give ourselves over to the re-formation of our character and conduct. With our souls open to correction, to instruction and to the new life of the Spirit we become people whom God Himself begets.

23

Then Peter got down out of the boat, walked on the water and came toward Jesus. But when he saw the wind, he was afraid and, beginning to sink, cried out, "Lord, save me!"

Matthew 14:30

Do you remember when you were first learning how to float? What was the greatest impediment to being able to remain on the surface of the water? If my memory serves me correctly, it was fear and distrust of the very element I was in relationship to.

Curiously, it is the very act of trying to brace yourself against the water that scuttles your ability to float. As you express your fears by flailing around, you invariably end up sinking. But once you relax, the very same water that seemed impossible to float in now becomes buoyant. It is almost as if the properties of water have changed according to your relationship to it.

This same phenomenon also applies to the life of faith. When we are trying too hard to secure ourselves, everything feels as thin as air. There seems to be nothing to hold on to. But once we relax and trust life to support us, like water, it suddenly seems thicker, more substantial.

We assert our confidence in God's faithfulness by relaxing in the disposition of trust. And, as Peter discovered, it is this very disposition that allows the water to then support us. To flail in our thoughts or to try to control our buoyancy in other ways will only increase the likelihood of our faith being scuttled by the fear of sinking.

We all begin our journey with the simple faith that God exists. But it is trust that God is good and that He undergirds our lives that then transforms this faith into the confident experience of certainty that it is meant to be. Only by fully trusting in the buoyancy of God—in whom we live, move, and have our being—will we ever come to appreciate just how supportive our faith really is. And, like the kid who cheats during swimming lessons by keeping one foot on the bottom of the pool while going through the motions of swimming, we will discover that anything less than the real thing is ultimately unsatisfying.

24

Devote yourselves to prayer, being watchful and thankful.

Colossians. 4:2

So much good takes place in the mysterious environment of prayer. So many wrongs are set right. So many new foundations are laid. As I consider the many benefits of prayer I am so thankful to God for the countless graces that I can attribute to this most effortless of disciplines. From the wellspring of its daily renewal I get to drink deeply of God's truth, purpose, and direction for my life

Prayer is where I get to examine all the different aspects of my life in light of the Lord's counsel. In prayer I find my Way—instructions for my day, and for my life. There, God teaches me new truths and reminds me of ones I have forgotten. There, the Holy Spirit identifies whatever tendencies there are in me that obstruct His Way.

In prayer I defer all the considerations of my life to God. I assume more readily the posture of a servant rather than that of a labourer for God. Like Mary who saw herself as the handmaiden of the Lord, I wait in order to let God's will be more freely expressed in me. Prayer is where I receive the relationship that God most desires to have with me.

In prayer I get to observe how I relate to all the different people and circumstances that surround me. I discover how I really feel about life. I get to sort through and re-establish my priorities—what God is calling me to, and what He is not. I also come to recognize my most profound desires as well as the fears that often influence my response to life.

Prayer helps me let go of the anxious grip I tend to otherwise hold myself with throughout the day. It loosens my fears, my worries, and the many burdens I've unnecessarily assumed for myself. If only for those few moments, everything stops. I know that I have returned to a place that has much more to do with eternity than the turmoil I have otherwise been living in.

In prayer I once again lay down my life before God. It belongs to Him and I enter the freedom whereby I am able to give myself more fully to the Lord's purposes. In doing so, I return to my most simple sense of self. There is nothing to do, no one to be, and nowhere else to look for myself than where I am. The only horizon I seek is the one right in front of me. Instead of the illusion that life is something I possess, I am once again reminded that it is actually something that is given to me. Moment by moment, I get to offer it all back to God in gratitude for the relationship I am in.

In prayer I place myself in the hands of the Potter, ready to be fashioned in any way that pleases the Lord. I try to remain malleable to God's will and to wherever the Holy Spirit might lead me in my prayer. Whatever Jesus is in me, that is what I wish to be. In this submissive posture I learn much about the ways of God.

And finally, at its most sublime, prayer is where I get to pull away from my usual orbit of self-reference in order to simply gaze at Jesus. In the solitude of prayer, all other definitions of my life pale in comparison to the wonder of contemplating the beauty of God's ways.

For this brief moment I am all I have ever been.
Nothing more, and so much less than
my anxious thoughts demand.
Here, I realize that
I am smaller than I think,
less than I imagine,
simpler than I ever dreamt.
I am the mustard seed from which
all beginnings stem.
I am the future I have not yet conceived
and the place of final rest that I hadn't expected
this soon.

25

You need to persevere so that when you have done the will of God, you will receive what he has promised.

Hebrews 10:36

My wife and I have now walked over 1500 km on the Camino de Santiago in Southern France and Northern Spain. If nothing else this 12th century pilgrimage route is a sustained exercise in perseverance.

This is a word that often came to mind in the midst of physical weariness, blisters and the heat of an afternoon sun.

Perseverance simply means to continue steadfastly and its Latin root implies that such steadfastness will often require *severus*—a strict "severity" of intention. It is a resolve that is otherwise easily challenged. The spirit of perseverance has life-long connotations for each one of us and it is good to recognize how the word applies to our physical and psychological capacities for forbearance.

Physical perseverance requires us to dig deeper than we normally would in order to stay with a task. It is an exercise in patient resolve, often carried out in a weary body that is more ready to quit than to carry on. It demands that we hold out longer than we think we can as we endure a discomfort. As a result, it also reveals to us greater limits of capacity than we ever knew we had.

Psychological perseverance is of a different order. It requires that we resist and find ways to counter the dis-couraging thoughts that often plague us as we trudge through a difficult terrain. How we think about our situation directly affects our capacity to endure what must be endured. Incessant "why?" or "how much longer?" questions only accentuate our discouragement. After suffering the ill-effects of such negative thinking for many days we eventually learn to cultivate a more positive psychology

Obsessing with finding an escape to our problems can also dissipate the spirit of perseverance in us. We are much more used to assuming that we can find a way out of a trial than in accepting that we must endure it. Whether it is difficulty in a relationship, in our circumstances, or even the trial of having to bear with ourselves for yet another day, there are many times in life when there really is no escape. We have no other recourse but to bear what must be borne.

For each of us, there will often be times in life when we are not called to overcome, to change course or to retreat, but to simply keep walking forward in the midst of our trials—to take one trudging step after another as we make our way through a difficult period. And it is in these times that we will come to better appreciate, not the God who rescues us from our tribulations, but the One who walks, one step at a time, along with us.

26

God forgave us all our sins, having canceled the written code,
with its regulations, that was against us and that stood opposed
to us; he took it away, nailing it to the cross.

Colossians 2: 13-13

There is a poignant scene in the 1998 movie *Les Misérables* that graphically illustrates the complex relationship between law and grace. It helps explain one aspect of why it was necessary for Jesus to die on the cross. The "written code . . . that stood opposed to us" has been nailed to the cross and we are now freed from whatever charges would otherwise be rightfully brought against us.

Victor Hugo's *Les Misérables* focuses on the life of ex-convict Jean Valjean as he struggles to be free from his debt to justice. Though he has repented from his life of crime and has become a force for good in the world, Valjean cannot escape his dark past. Throughout his life he assumes other identities in order to hide from the law that pursues him. Hugo embodies the "written code of the law" in the character of the obsessive police inspector Javert who relentlessly tracks Valjean so that justice might be satisfied.

At one point in the story, Valjean becomes implicated in the 1832 Paris uprising. Inspector Javert goes undercover behind the barricade in order to find and apprehend Valjean. But Javert is discovered by the resistance movement and his identity as a government agent is unmasked. Valjean is ordered to kill Javert, but chooses instead to let him go. This act of mercy, however, does not deter the relentless pursuit of the law as Javert continues to hunt him down.

Javert finally captures Valjean. But while waiting for the police wagon to arrive, he finds himself in an unexpected crisis of conscience. He is torn between his sworn duty to the law and the desire of his heart to grant the prisoner mercy. This conflict comes to a mysterious resolution when Javert inexplicably removes Valjean's handcuffs and lets him walk away. Only after the prisoner has escaped do we realize the drastic solution that has been reached. How can he let this man go free without negating everything he stands for—the very law that he has sworn to uphold?

There is only one solution possible and Javert accepts the full implications of his dilemma. He puts the prisoner's cuffs on his own wrists, and lets himself fall into the River Seine to drown. He who embodied all the charges that could be brought against Valjean has cancelled the debt owed to the law by removing himself from the equation.

In Hugo's novel, Jean Valjean represents the surprised recipient of grace. But it is Javert who curiously represents the Christ figure in this story. It was Jesus, after all, who similarly identified Himself as the law enforcer when He told us, "the Father judges no one, but has entrusted all judgment to the Son" (Jn. 5:22). But Jesus also declared His prerogative to offer mercy to all when He said, "I did not come to judge the world, but to save it" (Jn 12:47). Like Javert, Jesus accepts the radical implications that this choice represents for Him as the Righteous Judge. In order for mercy to reign, the law must die. Jesus, in a sense, ties His own wrists and lets Himself die on the cross.

Whether as an expression of human or divine sacrifice, this is what forgiveness always does. It removes the righteous demands of the law from the equation so that mercy can be freely given to those who are otherwise in debt.

Long my imprisoned spirit lay,
Fast bound in sin and nature's night;
Thine eye diffused a quickening ray—
I woke, the dungeon flamed with light;
My chains fell off, my heart was free,
I rose, went forth, and followed Thee.

—Charles Wesley (1707–1788)

27

In him (Christ) it has always been "Yes."

2 Corinthians 1:19

Throughout history, the spiritual path for many Christians has been largely defined in terms of renunciation of the world or of anything deemed unspiritual. It is called the via negativa. Through mortification of the flesh, self denial and abstinence, the spiritual life is understood as primarily against something. But others have walked a different path that is based much more on attraction than rejection. It is the via positiva, and St. Francis of Assisi is perhaps the best known example of this disposition.

Francis was motivated in his conversion not so much by what he stood against, but by what he sought. He fell in love, for instance, with the virtue of humility, welcoming opportunities for relationship with whatever might diminish him. Instead of suppressing pride he simply exalted humility. His approach to wealth was similar. Rather than condemn riches, he cherished the precious pearl of poverty. He embraced what he called Lady Poverty as one would cleave to a lover. In all this Francis exemplified the via positiva. Rather than curse the darkness of his sins, he simply lit the candles of their opposites. The via positiva affirms in us our desire for the things of God, and asserts our faith that "in Christ, all things are yes."

Our motivation for the spiritual life should always be a positive one. It should appeal to our desire for virtue rather than our abhorrence of vice, asking us who we want to be more than who we don't want to be. Love for something is a much more positive catalyst for change than the energy spent building up an aversion to the things we wish were different. This applies both to personal conversion as well as to social change. When we pursue something we love rather than counter something we hate, our vision is much more sustained in a spirit of hope. That is why gratitude also plays a key role in helping maintain a positive spiritual direction. Gratitude focuses our attention on what we affirm rather than what we disdain in our lives.

Francis did not see life as a problem to be solved but more as a hope to be attained. Humility, in his case, was not simply a way to counter his pride. He loved it for its own sake. What difference might it make for you to explore the Franciscan way in your own life—to pursue peace rather than flee turmoil, to seek gentleness and humility rather than rail against your anger and pride, to cherish holiness rather than try to solve the problems of sin in your life? In other words, how much more fruit would our spiritual lives bear if we let the positive vision of what we desire be our incentive for change more than the negative vision of what we don't want. It is easy to see how such an approach to faith would be much more attractive to us, and to others as well.

28

*Seek first the kingdom of God and all these things will be added
to you as well.*

Matthew 6:33

There are countless reasons why we should encourage one another to practice a regular discipline of prayer, and here are five that might inspire just that:

Prayer is the wellspring of renewed hope. Prayer is both the inspiration as well as the catalyst for change. It is usually in prayer where we become aware of the need, as well as the opportunity we have for transformation. Prayer is the most direct means we have of remaining malleable in the Potter's hand. In God's re-formation of our lives, we have opportunity to go beyond the limits of our own self-creation in order to become whatever the Lord has in mind for us. From such a re-creative state, it is easier to believe that all things are possible through God.

Prayer leads us to inner truth. Truth sets us free from the lies that bind us. In many ways we are all trapped by our misunderstandings or by the wrong assumptions we carry of ourselves, God and the world. Such lies distort us and often cripple the freedom that truth would otherwise produce in our lives. Prayer allows us to recognize the illusions we carry. It helps us identify and root out the things we are attached to that curtail our freedom, most of which are embodiments of our fears. Prayer is a place where such knots are disentangled by the Holy Spirit who loosens the grip they have on our premises.

Prayer teaches us the ways of the Lord. In prayer we have opportunity to discover and to explore more precisely the subtleties of our faith and its mysterious out-workings in our lives. As we closely examine God's relationship with us, we become more attuned to the "groanings" that take place within our spirits. We come to recognize our spiritual longings and the particular direction that these deep yearnings invite us to explore. Prayer is also where we come to express the longings that God has for others and for the world.

Prayer brings security and significance to the soul. Without prayer we become fearful in two particular areas of our lives—our need for security and for significance. When our lives feel unstable, we inevitably try to manufacture these existential needs for ourselves. Like the Israelites who felt lost without Moses near them, we create golden calves as substitutes for God. Daily re-establishing the assurance of God's sovereignty secures us existentially and removes the need for such idols in our lives. As our faith in God's initiative increases, so our anxieties and our need to control or protect our circumstances will decrease.

Prayer is the closest expression of our eternal relationship with God. And finally, one of the best reasons for spending time in prayer is simply because it expresses who we really are in this life. The posture that prayer produces in us best reflects our status as creatures who are still in the process of being created. No longer do we think of ourselves as the architects of our own lives and circumstances but, through prayer, we return to the more true state of our expressed dependence on God—the Creator who, each day, creates us.

By all means use some times to be alone
Salute thyself: see what thy
Soul doth wear
Dare to look in thy chest;
For 'tis thine own;
And tumble up and down
What thou find'st there.

George Herbert (1593–1633)

29

The goal is for all of them to become one heart and mind—
Just as you, Father, are in me and I in you,
So they might be one heart and mind with us.

John 17:22-23 (The Message)

Many of us operate from a much more dualistic sense of spirituality than we ought to. We tend to see and act as though God were wholly "other." We imagine our relationship with God as with One who accompanies us, helps us, counsels us, but who is ostensibly apart from us. How is this different from Jesus' relationship with His Father? And how does Jesus' prayer—that we would be one with God just as He and the Father are one—address this?

Mother Teresa was one among many saints who understood the spirituality of a life lived in tandem with God's movement. She taught her sisters the importance of this theology when she wrote,

> We must be aware of our oneness with Christ, as he was aware of his oneness with his Father. Our activity is truly apostolic only in so far as we permit him to work in and through us—with his power, his desire, his love.

Jesus told us plainly that, apart from Him, we can do nothing (John 15:4). Instead of seeking God for our marching orders, and then assuming the task of deploying these, we should rather seek, as Jesus did, God's direct movement within us as the very power by which we do all things. This is the gift of the New Testament whereby our obedience to God is to be sought through the impulse of the Holy Spirit, . As the Lord assures us through the prophet Ezekiel, "I will put my Spirit in you and move you to follow my decrees" (Ezek. 36:26-27).

Jesus offers the example of His own life as a model of the type of relationship we are to anticipate. Because He desires to share this oneness with us, Jesus prays that we would be united with the Trinity, just as He and the Father are. Mother Teresa reiterates this hope to her sisters and highlights its relationship to prayer.

> Our lives must be connected with the living Christ in us. If we do not live in the presence of God, we cannot go on. If you don't pray, your presence will have no power; your words will have no power.

No better definition exists for the nature of our unity with God than the one Jesus Himself offered when He said, "If you obey my commands, you will remain in my love, just as I have obeyed my Father's commands and remain in his love" (Jn. 15:10). Jesus' "commands" are simply the prompts of His indwelling Spirit moving us, from within, to be conformed to God's will. There is no other way to live the Christian life than in unity with Christ. Mother Teresa saw this as essential to anything we would call spiritual in our lives. She wrote,

Prayer is the very life of oneness, of being one with Christ. There-fore, prayer is as necessary as the air, as the blood in our body, as anything to keep us alive – to keep us alive to the grace of God. Ask the Holy Spirit to pray in you. Learn to pray, love to pray, and pray often. Feel the need to pray and want to pray.

The apostle Paul boldly declared that, "the life I live is not my own, it is Christ who lives in me" (Gal. 2:20). Can we say the same about ourselves? If not, what adjustments do we need to make in order for this statement to be true for us as well? The honest answers to these questions should make clear to us the spiritual direction we are being called to as we grow in our unity with God.

> *The whole progress of the soul consists in its being moved by God; but our own part remains in placing it in "a state to receive this motion"*
>
> St. John of the Cross.

30

> *Though you have countless guides in Christ, you do not have many fathers (or mothers).*
>
> 1 Corinthians 4:15

Many people involved with Imago Dei, including myself, meet regularly with a spiritual director. We have come to appreciate how God uses this ministry as a catalyst for our spiritual growth by keeping us on the narrow path of what our hearts desire most—union with God.

In his book, *The Contemplative Pastor*, Eugene Peterson describes his own relationship to the ministry of spiritual direction that, late in his life, he came to appreciate. He speaks of the initial motivation that first prompted him to seek a spiritual director.

> In looking for spiritual direction, I wanted someone who would take my life of prayer and my pilgrimage with Christ as seriously (or more seriously) than I did, who was able to hear the distinct

uniqueness of my spirituality, and who had enough disciplined restraint not to impose an outside form on me.

Paul, in his letter to the Corinthians, distinguishes between the many guides we have in the spiritual life and those who are more like spiritual parents to us in their mentoring. Peterson recognizes this distinction as well.

> It is easier to find guides, someone to tell you what to do, than someone to be with you in a discerning, prayerful companionship as you work it out yourself. This is what spiritual direction is.

Peterson also acknowledges the freedom that the objectivity of spiritual direction has brought to his own ministry.

> The first thing that I noticed after I began meeting with my spiritual director was a marked increase in spontaneity. Since this person has agreed to pay attention to my spiritual condition with me, I no longer feel solely responsible for watching over it. I found I trusted my intuitions more, confident that my self-deceit would be called to account sooner or later by my director.

In describing the pitfalls of a self-directed spiritual life, Peterson speaks for the predicament that many Christians find themselves in today. He writes,

> The problem in the past was that I was always the disciplinarian of my inner life, the one being disciplined, as well as the supervisor of my disciplinarian—a lot of roles to be shifting in and out of through the day. I was immediately able to give up being the supervisor, and was soon able to share the role of being the 'disciplinarian' with my director. In spiritual direction I no longer had the entire responsibility for deciding how to shape and monitor the disciplines in my life. I found myself more spontaneous, more free to innovate, more at ease in being nonproductive and playful.

Spiritual direction is a living, oral tradition. Though most directors might hesitate to see themselves as "parents," those who receive their ministry recognize that there is a big difference between being guided by a book or a person. As Peterson says,

> A Christian's need for personal spiritual direction cannot be delegated to books or tapes or videos. The very nature of the life of faith requires the personal and the immediate. If we are going to

mature we need not only the wisdom of truth, but someone to understand us in relation to this truth.

Such is the ministry of the spiritual "care of souls". It is not simply a matter of encouraging souls in general, but of specifically encouraging the unique soul of the person in front of you.

31

Remember that you were a slave in the land of Egypt and that the Lord your God freed you from there with a mighty hand and an outstretched arm; therefore the Lord your God has commanded you to observe the Sabbath day.

Deuteronomy 5:15

The Swiss theologian Karl Barth once wrote that a person is free only when they can determine and limit their activity. Barbara Brown Taylor, in her book, *An Altar in the World*, calls this the "practice of saying no." God calls it Sabbath.

For observant Jews, a proper Sabbath service begins on Friday evening the moment three stars can be counted in the darkening sky. It then calls for the lighting of two candles—one for each of the Sabbath commandments in which God's people are called to be more like God. They represent a candle of rest and a candle of freedom.

The first Sabbath candle reminds us that, since we are made in God's image, we too are called to rest as God does, and that we are to consider this form of rest as something holy. As Moses commanded the Israelites,

> Observe the Sabbath day by keeping it holy, as the LORD your God has commanded you. Six days you shall labor and do all your work, but the seventh day is a Sabbath to the LORD your God. (Deut. 5:12-14)

For six days we are commanded to work, but on the seventh day we are called to return to who we are, independent of our work. The Sabbath is a day that calls us not to do more, but to be more. As Brown Taylor puts it, "No longer do we tear the world apart to make our fire. On this day heat and warmth and light must come from within ourselves." Speaking of her own Sabbath experience she writes,

I have made a practice of saying no for one whole day a week: no to work, to commerce, to the Internet, to the car, to the voice in my head that is forever whispering "More." One day each week, more God is the only thing on my list.

Of course everything around us, as well as much within us, resists, to our own detriment, the wisdom of this command, which brings us to the second Sabbath candle. This candle is lit to remind us that we are no longer slaves to the systems of life. The second candle stands for the second formulation of the Sabbath commandment in Deuteronomy 5. There the context of the commandment shifts from the creation of the world to the exodus from Egypt.

> Remember that you were a slave in the land of Egypt and that the Lord your God freed you from there with a mighty hand and an outstretched arm; therefore the Lord your God has commanded you to observe the Sabbath day. (Deut. 5:15)

We, as well, can often feel like slaves of an unrelenting system which recognizes us only in terms of our productivity. We too risk buying into this identity as we lose sight of who we are apart from the work we do. And we too sense our spirits often groaning to God for deliverance from the false masters, many of our own making, that enslave our lives. Brown Taylor writes of this cry of the soul in describing the plight of the Israelite slaves, and of their emancipation by God.

> God's people cried out to God and God heard them, sending Moses to free them from bondage in a land that was not home. Resting every seventh day, God's people remember their divine liberation. That is what the second Sabbath candle announces: that, made in God's image, you too are made to be free from the excessive demands of this world.

The second candle represents the liberty that Karl Barth envisioned— the freedom to determine and limit our activities. Slaves are those who have lost such freedom in their lives. Speaking of the long-term fruit of establishing limits to our activity, Brown Taylor adds,

> Practicing it over and over again they become accomplished at saying no, which is how they gradually become able to resist the culture's killing rhythms of drivenness and depletion, compulsion and collapse. Worshiping a different kind of God, they are shaped

in that God's image, stopping every seven days to celebrate their divine creation and liberation.

As Jesus taught us, we cannot serve two masters. Sabbath-keeping is what helps us choose, in the long term, which master we will serve and therefore which identity we will claim for ourselves. One way or another, our image will reflect the character of the master we choose.

32

Just as he who called you is holy, so be holy in all you do; for it is written: "Be holy, because I am holy."
1 Pet. 1:15-16

The vocation of holiness is not something we often hear discussed among Christians in our day. For some reason it seems to be a value that we have relegated to a past age, a quality that we no longer expect from ourselves in the same way our forebears did. And yet the call to a sanctified life is no less imperative today than it was in past generations. The Lord still commands that we be holy for the simple reason that He, in whose image we are made, is holy.

Among contemporary advocates of holiness Mother Teresa perhaps most readily comes to mind as this is a theme that repeatedly shows up in her writings. In *Come Be My Light*, a compilation of letters written to her spiritual directors and various convents, Mother Teresa defines holiness in the most simple terms as she encourages her sisters saying, "Let us try to come as close as the human heart can come to the Heart of Jesus." This is the essence of holiness—to be as close as possible, in identity and in action, to the heart and person of Christ. In this we seek to reflect the sanctity that belongs to Him alone.

Biblically speaking, to be holy is to be consecrated, set aside for God. It is an act of self-offering in which we invite the holiness of God to express itself in our lives. Our motivation towards holiness comes from our love of God, but we can also be motivated by our love for others, as well as for the integrity of the Church. Mother Teresa writes of her own motivation to this vocation,

I am determined to show my love for the Church by becoming very holy. I ask you as well—please, for the love of God and the love of others take the trouble to be holy.

Mother Teresa lists three offerings on our part that contribute to the consecration of our lives to God: the offering of time, of will, and of our submission to others. She speaks of time set aside for prayer as a first priority, more important even than our ministry, or our relationship with others. Regarding her own experience she writes, "I always make my holy hour with Jesus straight after Mass, so that I get the first two hours of each day with Jesus. Before people and the sisters start using me, I let Him use me first."

Her desire for holiness comes from her deep love for the integrity of the Church. She also finds motivation in her love for others and from her desire to give as much as she can to those she ministers to. As she plainly states, "people are hungry for God. What a terrible meeting it would be with our neighbour if we give them only ourselves." Elsewhere she writes,

The more we receive in silent prayer, the more we can give in our active life. We need silence to be able to touch souls.

The second offering that Mother Teresa encourages from her sisters is that of the will. In submission to God, she sees all circumstances in her life as coming from the freedom she has given to God's will. She encourages this same disposition in her sisters when she writes, "I pray for you that you let Jesus use you without consulting you." In her own experience of submission she revels saying, "Today I have made a new prayer—Jesus I accept whatever You give—and I give whatever You take."

And finally, the third offering she encourages is that of our submission to others. In this Mother Teresa sees an action that is synonymous with submitting to God. She exhorts her sisters saying, "I only ask you to love one another as Jesus loves each one of you—for in loving one another you only love Jesus."

Such offerings, placed on the altar of consecration, express our desire that God would make of our lives a sacred place for His activity. Our own actions are then more able to reflect something of the holiness of the Spirit to whom we are submitted. Because God is holy, we can realistically hope to see this holiness mirrored in ourselves.

33

Make every effort to enter that rest.

Hebrews 4:10

What is the effort we must make in our prayers in order to enter God's rest? And when does that effort become a substitute for faith, usurping it with works? Perhaps comparing the "effort to enter that rest" with the mysterious phenomenon of sleep might help us recognize the relationship between the two.

When I was a child, for some reason I was fascinated with the idea of falling asleep. I would actually try to observe the exact moment when we pass from wakefulness to sleep. I'd feel myself getting drowsy and then, just when I thought I was about to fall asleep, I would try to catch myself, as it were, in the act. Needless to say I spent many nights awake as it is impossible to both fall asleep and to observe yourself doing so at the same time. Perhaps there is some similarity here with the un-self-conscious relationship we are invited to in contemplative prayer.

With little effort you can put yourself in a disposition that is conducive to sleep. You can drink a glass of warm milk, lie down comfortably, close your eyes, count sheep, whatever helps. But that is the most you can do. Eventually you have to give yourself over and let sleep come and take you to itself. The phrase "falling asleep" well describes the passive relationship we have to its final phase. You can lead yourself towards sleep but ultimately it has to come and take you to itself.

In some ways this is similar to the grace of stillness that we seek in contemplation. The most we can do is put ourselves in a disposition to receive it. We can be present to God, still our minds and try to be submissive as we open ourselves to the action of the Holy Spirit, but ultimately, only God can initiate the grace of prayer that will lead us to rest in His presence. The final act of "entering that rest" is something that only He can bequeath.

To "make every effort to enter that rest," as it applies to prayer, means to simply make ourselves available to God. The most we can do it to present ourselves on the altar of prayer in faith that the Lord will accept our offering. Once we have done this much we can do nothing more than wait as we anticipate God's invitation to go deeper. Like the mysterious gift of sleep, we can only "fall" into prayer as the Holy Spirit leads us. Like a ferryman, He meets us at the shore of our humble efforts in order to transport us, by His own vessel, to God's other shore.

There should always be more waiting than striving in a Christian's prayer.

— Evelyn Underhill

34

I applied my heart to what I observed and learned a lesson from what I saw.

Proverbs 24:32

Socrates' aphorism that "an unexamined life is not worth living," reminds us of the importance of taking time to reflect on the nature of our existence. This same wisdom can also be applied to our relationship to prayer. Taking time to reflect on our experience of prayer will give us opportunity to study and to more deeply relish this most mysterious of human activities.

Sports teams, performing groups, or businesses all place a high value on "post-event" evaluations as a way of learning how to make adjustments for better gain in the future. St. Ignatius of Loyola recognized as well the importance of a time of review following prayer as an essential part of our spiritual learning. He wrote,

After a prayer is finished, I will consider how I succeeded in the contemplation. If poorly, I will seek the cause of the failure; and after I have found it, I will make amends, so that I may do better in the future. If I have succeeded, I will give thanks to God, and the next time try to follow the same method. (S.E. 77)

Asking ourselves a few simple questions as we review our experience of prayer can become the very school from which we learn best how to pray. What seemed to help me in my prayer today? What hindered me?

What, from what I have learned, might I do similarly or differently in my prayer tomorrow?

Bill Clarke S.J., one of the spiritual directors at Loyola House, has come up with some other questions to help us reflect more productively on what our prayer experience has communicated to us. Following our time of prayer, Fr. Clarke asks us to reflect on what we experienced during prayer by asking ourselves questions such as these:

- How was I feeling during this time of prayer? (i.e., quiet, still, engaged, enthusiastic, fearful, restless, agitated?)
- What was my mood at the beginning of my prayer? At the end?
- What was I hoping for in my prayer? Did I receive it?
- If not, what other grace might I have received instead?
- What particular aspect of my prayer seemed to attract me today?
- What happened in me when it caught my attention?
- What, in particular, did I notice about God in my prayer? What was God's presence like?
- Did God seem close to me or far away?
- Did prayer reveal something new to me about God? About myself?
- What did I learn about the nature of this relationship?
- What is God inviting me to respond to?
- Is this prayer finished? Or is there something God wants me to go back to the next time I pray?

A "post-event" evaluation of our experience of prayer can be a formative tool for cultivating awareness through which God can lead us in our growth. We would do well to take a few minutes after we pray to explore its benefits for ourselves.

35

Oh, the depth of the riches of the wisdom and knowledge of God! How unsearchable his judgments, and his paths beyond tracing out.

Romans 11:33

Etch-ing (ech´ing) n. 1. A process of engraving in which grooves are made onto a metal plate, either scratched with a needle or by the corrosive action of acid. The grooves are then filled with ink and pressed onto paper.

Years ago I took a course in etching and learned an important lesson about my relationship with God. It had to do with the deepening initiative of God's love in my life and my feeble efforts to resist it. As I was working with a particular method of etching I recognized something very similar to the dynamics of my spiritual life.

In this form of etching, a metal plate is covered with beeswax. Once the wax has hardened, a fine needle is used to draw an image by scratching through the dried wax and exposing the bare metal. The resulting line is as thin as one could ever hope to draw. Once the drawing is finished the plate is then dropped into an acid bath. The acid etches the exposed parts of the metal, whereas the waxed parts are protected from the acid. The deeper the acid etches into the metal, the more ink the groove will hold, making a darker line on the final paper print.

As the metal is exposed to the acid an interesting phenomenon of oxidization takes place. The metal reacts to the acid and bubbles begin to form all along the lines of the drawing. This represents a minor problem for the artist as these bubbles create a protective layer over the line, preventing the acid from etching any deeper into the metal. If the artist wants the lines in the drawing to etch deeper, the bubbles must be removed with a feather, passing it gently over the plate. Once the bubbles are removed, the metal is once again exposed to the acid, allowing it to continue its deepening work.

As I observed the slow process of the acid etching into the metal I recognized how similar this was to the action of God in my life. As I watched the protective bubbles form over the lines I could see a similarity to my own ways of creating protective layers in my relationship with God—layers that shield me from the deepening action of love. And as the feather gently removed the bubbles from the line, exposing the metal once again to the acid, I also recognized the similar action of God's hand gently removing the bubbles I use as a shield against His intimacy. Though God's action exposes me to the very thing I am resisting, I know that the Lord does so in order that love might be etched more deeply in my life.

36

He will bring glory to me by taking from what is mine and making it known to you.

John 16:14

People being introduced to the themes of spiritual direction often feel like they are learning a new language. The vocabulary seems to speak deeply to their experience of spirituality, but differently than other ways they have been taught. It is a language that uniquely touches the heart. In one of his lectures on spiritual direction Eugene Peterson outlines some of the characteristics of this distinctive voice.

Peterson recognizes how the church, over the centuries, has evolved three manners of speech, known by their Greek names as *kerygma*, *didache* and *paraklesis*. *Kerygma* is the language of proclamation. Something has happened. God has entered the world. Jesus lived, died and rose again. As Peterson puts is, "This is not the vocabulary of abstract truth or ideas. It is a language that announces the fact that an event has taken place much like newspapers use kerygmatic speech to give the details of current events." *Kerygma* is, of course, central to the Christian witness. That is why we have pulpits, evangelists, missionaries and tracts.

Working alongside the kerygmatic speech of proclamation is that of *didache*—teaching, or didactic speech. Teaching is based on the premise that what has been revealed is capable of being understood. *Didache* is truth-telling, and it too has its place in the communication of our faith. As Peterson emphasizes, "There's rationality to what we are doing. Our minds function in some sort of correspondence to the mind of the Maker. There is a "Way" and it is a way that can be taught and learned."

Kerygma and *didache* are, of course, pillars of Christian communication. They present us with the objective truths of the faith. But there is another essential voice that is much more immediate and more personally related to the listener. It is the language of spiritual direction and, as Peterson emphasizes, it is a voice that the church desperately needs to recover—the language of *paraklesis*.

Parakletic language has to do with who and where we are in our experience of God. It addresses the realm of ordinary day-to-day life where the subtle work of discernment, obedience and sanctification is taking place. It speaks of our participation with the ministry of the Holy Spirit—the *Paraklete*.

Paraklesis is about the everyday world that Christians live in long after their initial conversion. The ministry of spiritual direction helps us appreciate how this realm is just as essential as anything that takes place from the pulpit or the lectern. It reminds us that, in the ordinariness of our lives, the gospel is incarnate in the details of who we are.

Paraklesis addresses the totality of our way of being—everything we share as humans. And we cannot live the Christian life nor achieve maturity in our communities, if we are not versed in it. It is the language with which we speak to one another about the spiritual realities we experience. Peterson adds, "We desperately need to recover maturity in our Christian communities and we cannot do it if all we know how to do is preach and teach."

Compared to proclamation and teaching, the language of spiritual direction is gentle, intimate speech. But it addresses the essential matters of our shared experience as Christians. Through *paraklesis* we learn to speak in the vernacular, where the truth of what has been proclaimed and taught is now being assimilated in our lives and in our communities.

37

Search me, O God, and know my heart;
test me and know my anxious thoughts.
See if there is any offensive way in me,
and lead me in the way everlasting.

Psalm 139:23-24

Spiritual transformation begins with confession, which is a simple matter of agreeing with God about any need for change He has indicated. This Scripture provides us with a model of how to open ourselves, in an ongoing way, to this process of spiritual re-direction in our lives. To simply ask God each day "if there is any offensive way in me" is one of the sure means by which the Lord will lead you in the "way everlasting."

To call the scrutiny of God upon yourself is to be mature enough to understand the purposes of God's sanctification and to be eager enough to want to participate with them. It is like an employee who, at the end of the day, asks the supervisor to point out all the areas in which he or she might improve, so that they can be a better worker tomorrow. Or like wise students who expect their piano teacher to serve them, not by overly praising or affirming their playing, but by helping them see, each week, where their playing is flawed. In other words, it is a sincere desire to uncover the many hidden errors that we cannot detect for ourselves.

Such an invitation certainly goes against the grain of our normal preferences for self-direction. It also robs us of the convenient hiding place of self-denial. When it comes to knowing our own faults most of us are much more willing to accept that "ignorance is bliss." We can barely keep up with the changes we already know we have to make. Why would we ask God to add things to this list we haven't even considered yet?

What type of person would pray such a prayer? Only those who are suspicious enough of their own self-serving scrutiny and who are prepared to accept that the only judgment that really counts is whatever God pronounces. As God judges me, so I am. In matters of what heaven considers offensive or not, we do well to not lean to our own understanding.

38

Truly you are a God who hides himself, O God and Savior of Israel.

Isaiah 45:15

There is a stage in a child's development that researchers recognize as one of infancy's most significant foundations. It is the capacity to retain the knowledge of something that has been hidden from sight, which usually develops in infants between eight or nine months old. The field of cognitive development calls this the capacity for object permanence.

Object permanence is the understanding that something continues to exist even if it can no longer be seen, heard, or touched. If we failed to develop this capacity, objects or events would have no separate, permanent existence of their own, and no relationship to us other than in the present moment. There are three stages in its development that offer helpful insights into the growth of our own capacity for object permanence when it comes to the presence of God in our lives.

In the first stage of developing object permanence, once an object is removed from a baby's view the infant might, at first, continue to look at the place where the object was. But its attention soon turns elsewhere. In its relationship to the outside world, the adage of "out of sight, out of mind" fully applies. This could well describe our early stage of maturity with regards to the presence of God. We are awakened to the fact of God whenever we recognize evidence that suggests the presence of His hand in our lives, but we soon fall asleep to this fact once that evidence is no longer tangible.

At a second stage of development a baby will reach out for an object that is partially hidden. The infant recognizes that the object is still there, even if it is not fully visible. This is perhaps the stage most of us find ourselves in with regards to our relationship with God. We recognize the signs of Divine initiative that are hidden in life. From these glimpses we then conjecture the reality that is implied—that God must somehow be hidden behind these signs.

At a later stage of development, a baby will search for a desired object even if it has been fully hidden from view. The infant knows that the object exists even though it is no longer visible. The child will usually look to where the object was last hidden, even if it is now somewhere else. It will then look elsewhere, hopeful of finding what it now recognizes as something that truly exists, even though it is hidden.

Parents, of course, have contributed to the development of object permanence in young babies for years. Games of peek-a-boo with a three month old are delightful because the child is so pleasantly surprised each time the parent hides their face in their hands and then suddenly "reappears." Does God similarly delight at our sense of surprise every time He suddenly "reappears" in our lives?" Children over five or six months will often reverse this game. They hide under a blanket and expect that their parents can't possibly find them, since the child cannot see the parent. Is this a game that we also play with God at times?

And finally, there is a curious downside to this acquired capacity that also parallels the maturing of our spiritual growth. Before object permanence is developed, a baby will not necessarily cry when the mother leaves the room. At around eight months however, the child will more likely show signs of separation anxiety whenever the mother leaves. The child now realizes that something it once had is gone—the presence of its mother. This also relates to our own maturing relationship with God as we often experience a form of separation anxiety when we feel that God has "left the room."

David once compared his relationship to God to that of "a weaned child with its mother" (Ps. 131:2). It speaks of the mature disposition of faith that God is inviting us to. May we, like a weaned child, learn to rest in the assurance that God is always present with us, even when He seems hidden from view.

> *God did this so that we would seek him and perhaps reach out*
> *for him and find him, though he is not far from each one of us.*
>
> Acts 17:27

39

I will not let you go unless you bless me.

Genesis 32:26

God seems to unfold His purposes in us, to some degree, according to the tenacity of our desires. As desire is sustained over time it reveals to us the worth of the things we hope for. Our tenacity in relationship to something, in other words, is an obvious indicator of the value we place on it. Its value ultimately shows up in our willingness to either persevere or give up on our hopes.

God, it would seem, not only recognizes our tenacity with regards to our true desires, but actually affirms and rewards it. We see this in the story of Jacob who wrestled with the angel of God all night long and would not let go until he had received a blessing. His tenacity was rewarded by the transformation of his very name.

The Lord often encourages His purposes in us through an initial infusion of love and joy that He places in our hearts. This first impetus is what is sustained in our subsequent desires to reach out towards the promise implied in that original invitation. Our persistence, coupled with faith in its fruitful outcome, is what we ultimately bring to the process.

E.M. Bounds, a 19th century preacher, once wrote,

> It is zeal, propelled by desire, that burns its way to the throne of grace and obtains its petition. It is the persistence of desire that gives triumph to the conflict in a great struggle of prayer. It is the burden of a heavy desire that sobers, makes restless and reduces to silence the soul that has just emerged from mighty wrestlings.

The story of the Syrophoenician woman is another object lesson that Scripture offers us to demonstrate the fruit of zealous desire (Mark 7:24-30). Though seemingly rebuffed by Jesus Himself, the woman was undeterred. With her face set like a flint, she let herself be moved by the inner imperative with which she had first begun her quest. Her desire was unstoppable in its intensity and unyielding in its boldness. And her tenacity was rewarded with healing.

On another occasion, Jesus used the parable of the persistent widow to teach how desire gains its end through obstacles that would otherwise impede weaker motives (Luke 18:1-8). In this case, the widow's tenacity was rewarded with justice.

There is an important lesson in each of these stories that speaks to us of the passion, or half-heartedness, with which we approach the things we hope for. Desire kindles the soul and holds it to the thing it is seeking. It exalts one thing over another.

As our desire becomes more specific it also becomes more intense. It might only want a few things, but it wants them badly. E.M. Bounds comments that,

> Too often our prayers operate in the dry region of a mere wish. Desire must be made intensely personal and directed to the hand of God to provide satisfaction. Without desire there is no burden of soul, no sense of need, no passion, no vision, no strength, no glow of faith. There is no mighty pressure, no holding on to God with a deathless, despairing grasp, "I will not let you go, unless you bless me."

It would seem that the indispensable requirement for all true praying, and for sustained spiritual growth, is a deeply seated desire that advances towards God in hopeful anticipation of its purpose. The Lord encourages us to be tenacious. As E.M. Bound concludes, "true desire is something that will remain unsatisfied until the choicest gifts in heaven have been abundantly gained."

40

Consecrate yourselves and be holy, because I am the LORD your God. Keep my decrees and follow them. I am the LORD, who makes you holy.

Leviticus 20:7-8

In these verses we see outlined the two major movements by which the spiritual life is advanced. They represent both our own initiatives, as well as God's power to sanctify that which is offered to Him.

Consecration is the human side of holiness. It is the voluntary and consistent dedication of one's self to God. Through it we set apart all we have, all we are and all that we hope to be as an offering for the Lord's use. In response to our self-consecration the Lord then promises to sanctify us. The divine action of the Holy Spirit working in our hearts purifies our lives, thereby producing the fruits of the Spirit in and through us.

God does not consecrate us to His service. That is something that only we can choose to do. But neither do we sanctify ourselves. That is something that the Holy Spirit promises to do with those who are consecrated to God.

The life of prayer naturally leads to an increasingly consecrated life. Prayer not only inspires a person to desire a consecrated life but it also sustains this objective as the focus of our spiritual direction. Without the support of prayer, the life of holiness breaks down. We find ourselves instead pursuing lesser faith objectives.

Prayer initiates as well as sustains the very imagination that inspires us to consecrate our lives to God. It helps consecrated Christians maintain their attitude of consecration. As we increasingly offer the ground of our being to God, prayer will keep us alive to the Holy Spirit who, each day, elicits this offering from us.

> *The Holy Spirit dwells in our hearts and whispers constantly to each one of us, "Surrender yourself to God's will, in all simplicity."*

> —Brother Roger of Taizé

41

> *"Everything is permissible"—but not everything is beneficial.*
> *"Everything is permissible"—but not everything is constructive.*
>
> 1 Corinthians 10:23

At the end of our days we will all look back and realize how the countless choices we made served to determine the particular path of our lives—choices about what to keep and what to discard from the many options that life offered us. Having lived a life in which "everything was permissible" we will understand, with much clearer hindsight, how all things were not equally constructive. This being so, what criteria is there for wisdom today in the important decisions that will inevitably chart the course of our lives?

Ignatius of Loyola taught his disciples how to make choices according to what best serves God. In his *Principle and Foundation,* he offers simple guidelines to help us keep our deliberations in good perspective. We must always have in mind, he teaches, the ultimate reasons for which we have been given life—first, to praise and serve our Lord, and secondly, for the working out of our salvation through God's grace. In light of these ultimate goals he then proposes that all things on the face of the earth—material, as well as life conditions and opportunities—are simply to be seen as potential helps, enlisted to achieve the purpose for which we were created.

Ignatius exhorts us therefore to make wise use of the resources and conditions we've been given and to assess their value solely in light of these ultimate goals. He writes,

From this it follows that we are to use them (all created things) as much as they help us achieve these ends, and we ought to rid ourselves of them in so far as they hinder us in achieving them.

It is a simple grid of understanding whereby we assess the ultimate value of the choices we make according to one defining question—will they help us to praise God and grow in sanctity, or will they hinder us? No longer is the criteria for making choices solely a matter of weighing our own preferences, or determining what is most to our perceived advantage. We ask, rather, out of all the options available to us, which ones best serve the foundational principle of our lives—God's purpose in and through us.

Since other concerns are secondary, we now have freedom to see all things as equal in themselves. Their value is deemed only according to how they serve as a means to accomplish that to which we have been called. Ignatius goes on to suggest that we should therefore remain indifferent to all created things so that, on our part, we should consider all options—riches, poverty, honour, dishonour, even long life or short life—as equally able to serve God.

To chart our course according to what best serves God's purposes is the foundational principle that keeps us from being led astray by the many other considerations we bring to bear in making life choices. In the midst of "all things being permissible," it is the only way we can discern which ones, ultimately, are most beneficial.

Remove the dross from the silver, and out comes material for the silversmith.

Proverbs 25:4

42

As the man went eastward with a measuring line in his hand, he measured off a thousand cubits and then led me through water that was ankle-deep. He measured off another thousand cubits and led me through water that was knee-deep. He measured off another thousand and led me through water that was up to the waist. He measured off another thousand, but now it was a river that I could not cross, because the water had risen and was deep enough to swim in—a river that no one could cross. He asked me, "Son of man, do you see this?"

Ezekiel 47:3-6

Ezekiel's vision of the increase of water flowing from the throne of God is significant to the topic of spiritual direction as it relates this increase to our capacity or incapacity to be in control of the stream of water that surrounds our spiritual life. It's a helpful image and one that resonates quite accurately with our experience of life in the Spirit.

Ezekiel starts at the beach and describes the process of wading on the shores of God's water. When we are ankle-deep in such spiritual waters we can already sense that we are in the flow of God's presence. We feel its cool embrace around our feet. Like walking barefoot on the ocean shore we can enjoy the assurance of the surf, all the while knowing that we can easily jump back to the sand if a big wave happens to come along. There is a freedom of options that is made possible by the fact that only a small portion of our body is submerged.

As we venture further into the ocean, to the point where we are now knee-deep in water, our freedom of movement is curtailed. We are not only more aware of the water surrounding us but also of the resistance we meet as we try to wade in its currents. The closeness of its embrace around our legs forces us to slow our gait. To move one foot in front of the other requires more effort and we feel sluggish compared to when we were skipping along the shore.

As we move even deeper into the water we are now half-submerged and we realize that we have less and less control over our stability. The waves that lap at our waist seem to knock us over. At the same time, there is a rip current below us that threatens to lift us off our feet. We are aware how easily we could lose our balance and we are now concerned with doing whatever it takes to avoid falling into the water. And yet this would seem to be exactly where this is all leading to.

As we wade deeper yet, the water has now risen to become a "river that no one could cross." The only option left, if we are to pursue this direction any further, is to now swim. We must let go of the security under our feet and be prepared to now fully immerse ourselves in the water if we hope to cross to the other side.

In Ezekiel's vision, as it is in our spiritual life, learning how to swim is a lesson that is often forced upon us by the increasing depth of the river we find ourselves in. The amount of water that flows from God's throne will inevitably dictate the terms of engagement. And our maturity will be defined by how willingly we accept the fact that these waters are wider and deeper than our capacity to walk across them.

43

The good man brings good things out of the good stored up in his heart, and the evil man brings evil things out of the evil stored up in his heart. For out of the overflow of his heart his mouth speaks.

Luke 6:45

The heart is a reservoir that is just as full of opportunity as it is of danger. It is from the overflow of the heart that we respond to life. According to Jesus, the heart is also a place where the past is stored. We have, within us, habits of the heart— prejudices, wounds, biases, and desires that are always influencing our choice of behaviour, thought and speech. For this reason it is of benefit to every Christian to take time in prayer to closely examine what gets stored in their own heart.

Prayer leads, among other things, to honest self-examination. Soon after his conversion St. Augustine prayed, "O God, let me know myself, so that I may know you." He was convinced that the honest knowledge of one's self is inseparable from the knowledge of God. Prayer is the observation deck from which we note the subtle motivations that move us in our day. Through the daily practice of examining our hearts we have opportunity to uncover what has been stored there and to learn, if possible, how to modify its content.

In Ephesians 4:31 the apostle Paul tells us that we are to "get rid of all bitterness, rage and anger, brawling and slander, along with every form of malice." Jesus locates the residence of such spirits in the heart. All our negative behaviour comes from attitudes and inclinations that have long been stored (i.e. permitted to dwell) there. To get rid of them means to no longer give them residence.

Good things are also stored in our hearts. Dispositions and ethical habits that have been formed by choices made years ago, or that we were brought up to imitate, are deposits that we draw on as we act in this life. We can also be pro-active in what we choose to bank there. A morning prayer, for instance, can be a time for intentionally storing good in our hearts for the day ahead of us.

Allowing our hearts to be revealed to us through prayer will help us be more intentional in choosing what influences our behaviour. The idea of storage will also encourage us to carefully consider what we wish to deposit, or allow to dwell, in our hearts for future use. As we intentionally store good within us Jesus assures us that when we speak and act in the world the overflow of what is in us will also be good.

> *Above all else, guard your heart,*
> *for it is the wellspring of life.*
>
> Proverbs 4:23

44

The words I have spoken to you are spirit and they are life.
John 6:63

Meeting with people for spiritual direction has taught me many things about how the Spirit moves within any God-oriented conversation. Words related to our deepest hopes and desires touch our hearts in ways that quicken these very things we long for. Perhaps the word resonance best describes the dynamic action of such words within us. Whether spoken or read, whenever the "word of God" touches us it re-sounds within us like the vibration of strings in a musical instrument.

The resonating effect of words on our hearts is of course something that preachers have long recognized. We are physiologically moved by what we hear. Spiritual reading, or *Lectio Divina*, also applies that same principle to the slow reading of Scripture. In spiritual direction as well, we see how God-resonating words affect the heart much like a breeze blowing over coals. Both the director and the directee sense something glowing in the heart as the topic of intimacy with God fans the flame of our desires.

Through simple conversations we discover the particular presence of the Spirit, not only in ourselves, but in the hearts of others as well. To some, the topics of prayer, silence, and spiritual union with Christ have very little resonance with their life desires. Others, however, find deep identification in these themes. I have often seen tears well up in people's eyes when the topic of intimacy with God arises. Such movements of the Spirit reveal the deep, though often unspoken, longings in a person's heart.

Words search us out. Like a divining rod they bend our attention towards the hidden wellsprings that lay buried in the deep ground of our being. As we recognize these places in ourselves and in those around us, the particularity of our vocabulary will associate us with others who share a similar hunger for the spiritual life. Words will help identify spheres of fellowship as they articulate the themes around which like-hearted people gather.

Such is the mysterious power the Lord has given to simple words. They are God's principle instruments for identifying the Spirit's movement in us and in others. They create life as they quicken the heart; they focus the attention of our desires; and they gather us in our spiritual direction.

45

I am the Gate. Anyone who goes through me will be cared for—
they will freely go in and out, and find pasture.

John 10:9 (The Message)

For a person who seems so intent on pursuing unity with God I am always surprised at how much time I spend living, thinking and acting as though I were an autonomous being. My natural default is to presume that I am alone in the world. Even as a Christian I experience myself as being a citizen of two realities at the same time—one in which God is the centre, and the other where I am. Can both these worlds co-exist?

Many of us have resolved at one time or another to "practice the presence of God" as a daily rule for our lives only to find ourselves hopelessly forgetting to do so for most of the day. To try to remain constantly mindful of the Lord's presence seems to go against a natural grain that is quite entrenched in us to do otherwise. Should this be cause for guilt? Should we be surprised that we seem to prefer self-centeredness over a God-centered life? Or does Jesus assume and accept this as par for the course?

For many reasons, we all experience times when God seems to be absent. But more often, the reverse is true—it is *our* hearts which are absent from God. It is we who leave God for other pastures. As Bernard de Clairvaux confessed in the 12th century,

> Nothing can be so restless and fleeting than my heart. How exceedingly vain, trifling, wandering and unsettled is this vagabond. It is under a thousand different determinations all at once.

How does Jesus view such wandering? When I am concerned with how God judges my fickle heart I often take consolation in Jesus' description of the sheep who are free to go in and out of pasture. Jesus knows that, like sheep anywhere, we are guided mostly by our basic wants and needs. We return to the pasture when we're hungry and wander away when we aren't. Lucky for us, all this takes place under the watchful eye of our Shepherd who knows that we are never really very far from His gate.

A natural ebb and flow in relationships seems to be the norm wherever love is in motion. Even the angels in heaven are described as coming and going, like moths to a flame, to and from God's presence. Jacob saw as much in his vision of a stairway to heaven where angels both ascend and descend from the throne of God.

If we were ever capable of loving someone with unchanging constancy it would never offer the same dynamic quality as a love that oscillates freely between intensity and a more relaxed normalcy. The Lord, it would seem, expects us to go freely in and out of pasture. Absence, after all, is one of the very conditions that God has created in order to make the heart grow fonder.

46

In all the travels of the Israelites, whenever the cloud lifted from above the tabernacle, they would set out; but if the cloud did not lift, they did not set out—until the day it lifted. So the cloud of the LORD was over the tabernacle by day, and fire was in the cloud by night, in the sight of all the house of Israel during all their travels.

Exodus 40:36-38

Being brought up on the shores of the St. Lawrence river taught me a lot about the art of navigation as I used to often watch the large ships zigzag their way through the islands that dot the river from Montreal to Kingston. There is a method in how these ships are guided in this process that I have come to recognize as very similar to the way God uses vision to guide us in our lives.

In order to steer a ship safely around the islands, the captain is guided by lights on the shore towards which he must aim his craft. As he sets his sights towards one of these lights the ship appears to be heading towards that shore. Once they have made their way past the island however, another light comes into view on the opposite shore. The ship now changes course and steers towards the new guiding light until, once again, it reaches the point, past the next island, where another light on the opposite bank comes into view. Throughout this process, though the ship appears to be heading towards the light on the shore, this target only serves its purpose until the second light becomes visible—a light that would never have come into view had the ship not advanced in the direction of the first light.

God often guides us in similar fashion. We feel positive that we are being led in a certain direction only to find another option suddenly become evident to us—one that we would never have noticed had we not begun moving in the direction of our first objective. This can be disconcerting at times, especially if we've become attached to our first assumption.

As with the Israelites in the desert, wherever the Divine cloud lifts from above our tabernacle we know that the Lord is inviting us to break camp and follow Him. It is natural however, in times of spiritual movement, to try and second-guess God. We think we know where we are going and we start making plans for our arrival. Sometimes our foresight proves accurate, but often it is problematic. We want to participate with our assumptions of God's direction and we get confused when the cloud of Divine guidance stops, or suddenly changes course.

In their desert experience, it was apparent that the Lord was simply teaching the Israelites how to heel. When He moved, they moved. When the cloud stayed over them, they did not set out until it once again lifted. What appeared to be aimless wandering was, in truth, tutelage in the precision of obedience. It was an exercise in faithful obedience to the movements of God.

We too must learn that God often leads us by indeterminate ways. Sometimes He will use "lights" on the shore of our vision in order to move us forward to another position. But we should not assume these lights to necessarily be our final destination. In the course of our movement, we shouldn't be surprised if, for no apparent reason, the Lord suddenly seems to change our direction, or even stops us abruptly in our tracks. If we anticipate this as normal in the course of our spiritual direction, we will more easily welcome such changes in our plans as simply part of learning to be obedient to the often-unpredictable, but always purposeful, movements of God.

47

"Be careful, or your hearts will be weighed down with dissipation . . . and the anxieties of life."

Luke 21:34

At 6:10am, on the morning of Aug. 29th 2005, Hurricane Katrina hit the city of New Orleans with 145 mph winds. The ocean waters surged 18 to 25 feet above normal tide levels. By 8 a.m. the water had topped the levees. The entire city quickly became a flooded cesspool of toxic chemicals, human waste and debris as the outside waters breeched the protecting walls.

A few months later, investigators identified poor materials used in the construction of these levees as one of the main reasons for the breech. As the floods surged, the walls eroded in these weak spots and the city lost its line of defense. The lesson here, in tragic hindsight, was that the levees should have been inspected more often, and been more diligently maintained.

Whether it's your body's immunity system or the anti-virus program on your computer, like the levees around a city, we often depend on walls of protection to prevent unwanted aspects of the outside world from coming into the core of our systems. This same principle also applies to our spiritual life, especially to the ways that stress and worry often spill over and dissipate our hearts with anxiety.

Most of us don't have a real sense of separation between our inner self and the world outside. Our hearts often get flooded by whatever incoming waters surge over its walls. That which is outside finds its way to the inner chambers of our being. Like water being pumped out of a flooded basement, it then becomes a long and difficult process to expel these stresses from our hearts.

Prayer is the best means we have for building up the walls of our defense. It does so by strengthening the inner man or woman. It helps maintain the boundaries between the inner and the outer life. In so doing, it provides us with objectivity towards all the events and circumstances that surround us. Without such differentiation we are like corks bobbing up and down according to the waters of circumstance. But with this distinction in place, we are more able to wisely choose our actions and our responses to life.

Differentiation doesn't mean withdrawal from the world. It means remaining vitally connected to what is happening around us, while still retaining our sense of separation from it. Consider how this applies to your present experience of life. Are the levees of your heart well maintained? Do outside circumstances too often find their way into your inner sanctum? If so, how can you be more diligent about protecting your inner life from outside clutter? Our daily prayer time is key to our experience of a well-differentiated life.

48

*When the apostles returned, they reported to Jesus what they
had done. Then he took them with him and they withdrew by
themselves to a town called Bethsaida, but the crowds learned
about it and followed him.*

Luke 9:10-11a

In the week prior to this scene Jesus had sent His disciples off on their
first unaccompanied ministry tour. Luke 9:1 says that He gave them
"power and authority to drive out demons and to cure diseases." And, in
the power of Christ's name, that's exactly what they did. Now, wonderfully
triumphant on their return, they are excited to share with their Master
all that they had witnessed on their ministry tour. Jesus, perhaps sensing
this to be an important bonding time, suggests that they all go away on a
retreat together. He leads His disciples to a small town called Bethsaida.
Jesus has expectations of spending some quality time with His friends.

But, no sooner do they get there than they notice that the same crowd
that had been shadowing them for the past few weeks has now followed
them to Bethsaida. So much for their retreat. You can just imagine the
groaning in the disciples' spirits as they realize that they are about to lose
out on this special time with their Master. "'Go away!" "We're sorry. You'll
just have to come back later." "We have important things to discuss."
"This is our time!" "This is *our* Master!"

It's easy, as well, to imagine Jesus being justified in saying something
like "'My time is short. I must minister to those my Father has given to
me. They have much work to do after I depart." But this isn't at all what
the Lord says. The Master of the Universe has just had His plans derailed
but, since He is also the Master Improviser, it doesn't seem to bother Jesus
one bit. Luke 9:11b describes the Lord's response to this intrusion: "He
welcomed them and spoke to them about the kingdom of God, and healed
those who needed healing." No resentment, no impatience, no sense
of regret at having to allocate His resources away from one application
for the sake of another. How different is this from the way most of us
might've reacted to this situation?

How often do our best laid intentions get derailed by unexpected
turns? The plans are good. It is important that they get accomplished.

And then the phone rings. Or there's a knock at the door. Someone has a pressing need and expects you to immediately stop what you're doing to help them. How do you respond? "I can't help you right now." "I was going to spend some quiet time with Jesus." "You'll have to come back later, when I am finished with what I think God is calling me to do."

When our expectations are upset, it is important to remember that Jesus doesn't seem to overly mind having His plans interrupted. It could be that the Master Improviser also wants us to be as free as He is in dealing with the unexpected intrusions of life.

49

I tell you the truth, the Son can do nothing by himself; he can do only what he sees his Father doing, because whatever the Father does the Son also does.

John 5:19

I studied sitar for a number of years while I was in university. It's a beautiful instrument whose characteristic sound is shaped by twelve thin strings that lay below the main melody and drone strings. As a note is plucked on the melody string, the "sympathetic" strings below it, though unplayed, resonate with its vibration and create the uniquely familiar tone of the sitar.

A western example of this is an instrument that, for the purposes of this meditation, is aptly called the "viol d'amour." This is a violin-shaped instrument with seven gut strings that are bowed to produce the melody. Beneath them, another set of sympathetic metal strings vibrates in response to the bowed strings. A unique and beautiful sound results as the resonating strings work in concert with the melody string, receiving their sonic "cue" from it and responding sympathetically to its vibrations. It is no wonder that such an intimate relationship between the melody and the resounding strings inspired the name *viol d'amour* or "violin of love" for this instrument. The word *sympathetic*, which literally means "together with feeling," also applies.

A universe in perfect "sympathy" with its Creator's melody would be harmonious indeed. Everything would be in right relationship with its creative origin. But what if, instead of sym-pathy, each resounding string had a mind of its own. It would receive the original vibration of the melody string but could then choose whether to respond in kind or not. For its own assumed purposes, the resonating string could either quicken the vibration it received by adding its own impulse to it, or else dampen the original vibration by resisting its initiative. With sympathetic strings acting much less sympathetic to the original tone, you can imagine the discord this would produce. And yet this is a good description of what happens in the world, and within us, in relation to God's divine impulse. We do not purely re-sonate that which we have received from God.

In J.R. Tolkein's *Silmarillion*, this principle is told in the form of a fable. In this classic tale Tolkein offers a creation myth in which Eru, the Creator, forms a community of angels who are called "the offspring of his thought." Eru sings a Divine melody and then invites the angels to make great music with its theme. One of the angels named Melkor, however, rebels and uses his power to develop his own song, causing discord and division in the world. It is easy to see what Tolkein is implying here regarding our own dissonance with God's melody.

We too have contributed to the discord of Melkor in all our relationships by adulterating the theme that has been given to us. But thankfully, the original song cannot be lost. It continues to play its melody, inviting us to join it by becoming more and more like Jesus, who only sings what He hears the Father sing.

To desire to be more perfectly in tune with the Creator's song. To seek to re-sonate, in a pure and unadulterated way, the life that we have been given. To be sym-pathetic (i.e. together in feeling) with all that our Father is doing in and through us. This is the invitation that Jesus, the perfect pitch of salvation, sings to a discordant world.

50

This is what the Sovereign LORD says: "I will gather you from the nations and bring you back from the countries where you have been scattered, and I will give you back the land of Israel again. They will return to it and remove all its vile images and detestable idols. I will give them an undivided heart and put a new spirit in them."

Ezekiel 11:17-19

If the practice of prayer teaches us anything it certainly teaches us just how scattered we can be. If our intent in prayer is to present ourselves to God in a consolidated way, the exercise of prayer often serves to reveal just the opposite—how fleeting and dodgy our inner life really is. We are rarely "undivided" within ourselves, and it can be discouraging, to say the least, to have that impressed upon us repeatedly in our exercise of prayer.

As we seek to return to our true self—our "land of Israel"—it is natural that this will also occasion a heightened awareness of all the "vile images and idols" that have kept us scattered in other "countries." It would seem that this is a necessary first stage of our healing. As we grow in our awareness of just how strong our attachments are to these idols we come to more fully appreciate how any hope of return to our true self is impossible without God's grace and initiative. Only God can give us the undivided heart we need in order to seek and therefore find our true hope.

Thomas Merton once said, "If you want to have a spiritual life you must first unify your life." In other words, before we can offer ourselves to God we must first become united in the focus of who we are. This "turning" of our whole self to God is, as Merton adds, something that "can be achieved only by deep and simple faith, and a love which desires above all things to do His will." Like the focused rays of a magnifying glass, it is only by turning to God that we will ever experience such unity within us.

To gather all people together as a unified community before God is the declared intent of the Holy Spirit among the nations. To gather all the scattered aspects of our inner life into a graced whole before God is the same divine agenda applied personally. Whenever we respond to the *shema*—the call to "love the Lord your God with all your heart and with all your soul and with all your strength" (Deut. 6:5)—we participate with the promptings of this new spirit.

The beautiful disposition of a unified heart is what the Lord forms in us as He orients our lives towards faith and prayer. God promised His people that He would take the initiative to "give them an undivided heart and put a new spirit in them." We are encouraged by Scripture to believe that it is towards such a place of focused worship and prayer that our spiritual maturity is ultimately leading us. In the meantime we are to anticipate and grow in our longing for this fruit, even in the midst of learning just how incapable we are of establishing it for ourselves.

> *Teach me your way, O LORD, and I will walk in your truth;*
> *give me an undivided heart, that I may fear your name.*
> *I will praise you, O Lord my God, with all my*
> *heart; I will glorify your name forever.*

Psalm 86:11-12

51

> *My strength is dried up like a potsherd,*
> *and my tongue sticks to the roof of my mouth;*
> *you lay me in the dust of death.*

Psalm 22:15

Times of desolation are a normal part of every Christian life. Why we experience such seasons and how we should respond to them are important questions as we grow in the subtle art of spiritual discernment.

In his *Spiritual Exercises,* Ignatius described the experience of desolation as follows:

> Darkness of soul, turmoil of spirit, inclination to what is low and earthly, restlessness rising from many disturbances which lead to want of faith, want of hope, want of love. The soul is wholly slothful, tepid, sad and separated, as it were, from its Creator and Lord.

He then lists three reasons why God allows desolations to occur. The awareness of these might help us consider the important benefits that can also result from a right understanding of such seemingly fruitless experiences.

The first reason for desolation that Ignatius offers is that of spiritual correction. We are ripe for desolation when we become too attached to the world. When that is the case, God sometimes allows a spirit of dissatisfaction to afflict us in order to wean us away from our inordinate attachments to the things around us. Such attachments can easily detract us from following the Holy Spirit. In the Book of Revelation Jesus said to the church of Laodicea, "You say, 'I am rich; I have acquired wealth and do not need a thing.' But you do not realize that you are wretched, pitiful, poor, blind and naked" (Rev. 3:17). A spirit of desolation can help us realize the falseness of our situation by taking away the satisfaction we otherwise derive from it.

A second benefit of desolation is as a means of testing our faith. It challenges us with regards to our commitment to pursue God even in the absence of consolation. Consolation can be seen as a favourable wind behind us, helping us along. Desolation, then, is the afflicting wind in our face that resists our advance. In this opposing wind, our perseverance and determination to move forward are tested.

A third benefit of desolation is that it produces humility in us. When we can no longer, on our own, arouse feelings of devotion for God, we more realistically appreciate that these feelings that we have perhaps taken for granted are truly gifts from God and not the result of our own zeal. We realize that, left to ourselves, we cannot muster the fervour nor devotion to God that we desire. This is humbling and it helps us appreciate the poverty of spirit that is always our starting point for spiritual growth. When the wind is at our back it is easy to take credit for the smooth sailing, but when the wind stops we have a more authentic experience of who we are, and what we can or cannot do on our own.

Whenever periods of dryness come upon us it is good to consider whether the dryness is the result of disorder in our lives, or perhaps simply an invitation for us to mature in prayer. If we discern that the dryness is not the result of disorder, the Lord may be simply drawing us to a greater level of maturity—one that requires faithfulness despite the heaviness of spirit, or apparent loss of interest we may be experiencing. In this case we must be prepared to meet desolation head on and to persevere, resisting the temptation to set prayer aside.

The final encouragement that Ignatius offers is to remind us that desolations are usually temporary and must be understood in terms of the ongoing mystery of God's spiritual formation of our souls. Jesus assures us that His intention for us is joy (Jn. 15:11). Paul as well urges us to "rejoice in the Lord always" (Phil. 4:4-7) and in all situations (Phil 4:12-13). These and other assurances from Scripture tell us that we can expect desolations to be temporary aberrations from the normal ways God leads us in our spiritual direction.

52

The sun has one kind of splendor, the moon another and the stars another; and star differs from star in splendor.

1 Corinthians 15:41

One of the best articulations of the mystery of the Trinity that I have come across is in a book by Jeff Imbach in which he comments on the insights of John Ruusbroec, a 14th century priest and mystic. In *The Recovery of Love*. Imbach speaks of the profound nature of relationship found within the Trinity, where both unity and individuality are fully evident. Commenting on Ruusbroec's writings he describes how the perfect union found in the Godhead exists without compromising the particularity of its members.

> The Trinity is the movement of Persons toward an embrace of love in union so profound and so deep that there are no longer any distinctions between the Persons, only Oneness. At the same time there is a simultaneous and continual flowing out into fruitfulness and diversity, or plurality of Persons. It is this ebbing and flowing into union and into fruitful plurality that is the mystery of the Trinity—One yet Three.

St. John of the Cross observed that "love naturally desires unity with the object of its love." We know how true this is in our human experiences of love, and yet we also know how easy it is to lose our sense of differentiation within a relationship. We feel the need at times to pull back in order to reassert our particularity. This recoiling from relationship can seem at odds with the imperatives of love. But Imbach observes,

> Love cannot be simply self-sacrifice. Love is an exchange. People recovering from dysfunctional relationships know this. But they feel that the movement to establish their own personhood and create personal boundaries is contradictory to love. This movement to individuality feels necessary for survival, but at the same

time it seems to violate their understanding of love. Seeing love rooted in the Trinity gives people the much needed permission and courage to build their own sense of individuality as part of their growth in love.

Our own particularity is something that most of us have trouble accepting. Everyone else is similar but, somehow, we seem uniquely different. But the truth is, every human being experiences something of the burden of their own particularity. The question is whether we see this as a problem to solve, or as something to celebrate. To view it as the latter is to recognize that the uniqueness of who we are is an expression of the Trinity. As Imbach puts it,

> when we desire to make ourselves known in the world, to declare our distinction and uniqueness, and to form our own ego boundaries, we are, in fact, experiencing the impulse of Divine Love.

As star differs from star in splendour, so the Lord celebrates the uniqueness which He has created in each one of us—how we gloriously differ one from one another. Because we are made in the image of the One-in-Three our particularity is as much a cause for Divine celebration as is our place in community. Imbach explores the implications of this further when he writes,

> Love in the Trinity is both the passion to be One and the passion to be Unique. This is the other side of love. It is the passion to be a separate individual person. It is the dance of separateness, individuality, and diversity. The exchange of love in the Trinity is neither the embrace of union so total there is no distinction left, nor is it the celebration of separate persons. It is both, and both simultaneously, each flowing out of the other.

Only within the sublime mystery of the Trinity can the one and the many co-exist without compromise. In the context of such a marvelous truth, the splendour of our individuality, as well as the unity of Christian community, are both divinely affirmed.

53

Enter his gates with thanksgiving and his courts with praise; give thanks to him and praise his name.

Psalm 100:4

I was particularly blessed once with a word from my spiritual director about the importance of always anticipating good from God. This word gave me a new grid from which to interpret all the toils and troubles of my life. As I was bemoaning the circular nature of my spiritual struggles and the rut I had been in for most of the week she calmly said to me, "Remember Rob, that all things will end in gratitude." And she was right. Within a few days God led me to a place from which I clearly saw the benefit accrued from all my struggles. As I've since had many occasions to remember this wisdom I've found myself more and more assured that it applies to every difficulty we face. I try to remember in each of these trials that "all things will end in gratitude."

We often come through a difficult period and, while we might never wish to revisit that experience again, we are nevertheless grateful to God for it. We recognize that we have gained something important that could not have been ours by any other means. This happens over and over again in our lives. But if this is such a recurring pattern why aren't we more disposed to anticipate this end at the onset of our trials? Why aren't we more inclined, in the midst of our difficulties, to believe that, just around the corner, there is a place of respite from which we will be thanking God once again?

The Bible, in many places, anticipates the thanksgiving with which we will one day enter God's courts. The Book of Revelation speaks of the consolation that awaits us as God wipes away every tear from our eyes (Rev. 21:4). The Apostle John speaks of the mother who forgets all her labour pains once her child is born (Jn. 16:21). And Isaiah, in one of his most celebratory visions, pictures the consummate feast where, when all is over and done, the best of meats and the finest of wines will be served to all in attendance. At that time, when all manner of death and disgrace are forever removed from our experience, the prophet anticipates our grateful response. Regardless of the sufferings we have known in our lifetime, we will all join the chorus of thanksgiving saying,

> "Surely this is our God; we trusted in him, and he saved us. This is the LORD, we trusted in him; let us rejoice and be glad in his salvation." (Isa. 25:9)

All things will end in gratitude. Knowing this to be true helps us appreciate how being grateful today puts us immediately in the disposition we will enjoy forever in heaven. Hope lies in our anticipation of this, even in the midst of our present troubles. In all our trials we are wise to remember the song of praise we will sing along with all those who have suffered life, "We trusted in Him, and He saved us. Let us rejoice and be glad in His salvation!"

54

God is in heaven and you are on earth, so let your words be few.
Ecclesiastes 5:2

During a recent Imago Dei retreat on Quadra Island we stayed at the home of the facilitator of the ID group up there. One morning John and I were up early and, as everyone else was still sleeping, I suggested that it would be nice to have a time of silent prayer together before the hubbub of the day began. John, who lives alone, agreed and observed how rare it is for him to find such opportunities for intentional silence with others. I commented on the busy-ness of city life and then mentioned the wonderful depths of silence that I had been enjoying recently in my prayer life. John spoke as well of the solitude of his life on the island, where silence is often such a welcome friend. We went on like this (I probably did most of the talking) for the next half hour and it was only when the others finally awoke and joined us that we realized we had lost the precious opportunity to actually enjoy the silence we had so enthusiastically been talking about.

The idea of prayerful silence is certainly attractive. We enjoy discussing it, reading books about it, even singing songs about it. But when it comes to actually entering into intentional silence it is curious how we will use just about anything to avoid it. Silence requires absolutely nothing from us. Perhaps that is why it feels like such a waste of time.

In my explorations of stillness these days I am often challenged as I recognize my perpetual need to create and sustain the inner activity of my soul. There seems to be a deep psychological imperative, in the sounding board of my imagination, to utter non-stop words to myself, to others, and to God. And I recognize more and more that I do this as an alternative to simply being content with the silence of who I am. Silence is the simplest altar imaginable and yet I seem so intent on finding ways to avoid kneeling there.

When I contrast the flippant subject matter of most of my mental activity with what I know I truly desire in prayer I am embarrassed to admit that I actually choose to pursue such things rather than the silence of God's presence. Why are we so willing to substitute almost anything, no matter how trivial, for the stillness of prayer? This is what every saint must ask themselves if they are to learn how to rest in God's presence.

In silence there is nothing left to do, nothing left to be. We are completely unadorned. From this precarious place, in which nothing you do and nothing you are seem to matter, a fresh sense of freedom can be born—the easy yoke of a life that we are no longer responsible to create.

It is because of such precious moments of silence that the question of inner stillness has become more and more important to me. Having tasted something of its utter simplicity I feel attracted, more than ever, to this place of being. I recognize it as the truest expression of who I am.

Even if they last only for a few seconds, such experiences reveal the ontological "ground" of my existence. In those rare moments, when all inner chatter has stopped, life seems as small as a mustard seed. In the purity of such experiences, I believe I glimpse something of my most humble state. And, when all is said and done, that is the true sum of who I really am.

55

*The high places, however, were not removed; the people continued
to offer sacrifices and burn incense there.*

2 Kings 12:3

This phrase shows up numerous times throughout the first and second book of Kings, and the consequence of this chronic problem represents centuries of waywardness for God's people. The "high places" here refer to alternative altars of worship that drew the Israelites away from their God. The people of this time knew no peace and, to the Biblical writer, the reason was obvious—these distractions, which were supposed to have long been removed, still remained standing. Their continued presence served to confuse and misdirect the allegiance of God's people.

It would seem that this condition is one that still persists today. We too have many "high places" that draw our attention away from God. Alternative altars of worship lure us away each day and in every aspect of our lives. The subtleties of their influence become especially noticeable in prayer when we find ourselves unable, for many reasons, to focus our attention on God. The invitation to silence serves to reveal the countless diversions we seem to prefer to the presence of God.

There are times in prayer when twenty minutes or a half hour can feel excruciatingly long, something akin to watching paint dry. Restlessness mounts and a low-level anxiety causes a strong desire within us to be doing absolutely anything else. We feel desperate for an alternative. We find ourselves climbing the walls of our mind, ready to latch onto any distraction. Such experiences serve to highlight just how addicted we are to the active life. The discomforts we feel at these times are evidence of withdrawal symptoms. And this should be proof enough to convince us that these "high places" are problems that must be removed.

What exactly are we addicted to in our thoughts? It could be anything from "the importance of being me" to "the problem of being me." From petty concerns to major fears. From whatever I want at the moment, to worries over the things I am trying to avoid in life. All these concerns represent the many pulls of the ego as it tries to establish the priority of its focus above all others. Such are the habits of self-reference that have always kept us from turning to God.

As we see these "idols" in terms of our addiction to self, prayer then becomes a place where we have opportunity to dry out. The discomfort of withdrawal that takes place in silent prayer is not much different than what happens in a detox centre. In the detoxifying environment of contemplative prayer the center shifts—the importance of self decreases so that the importance of Christ might increase.

It is not an easy process to wean ourselves away from an active mental life but it is essential that any high place that competes with our desire to seek God be removed. As Paul put it, we must contend against "every pretension that sets itself up against the knowledge of God, and take captive every thought to make it obedient to Christ" (2 Cor.10:5). In other words we must turn away from the sin of idolatry that our preferred option towards self represents.

56

For this reason a man will leave his father and mother and be united to his wife, and the two will become one flesh. This is a profound mystery—but I am talking about Christ and the church.

Ephesians 5:31-32

Ballroom dancing is a beautiful thing to watch. The synchronicity of a couple gliding effortlessly on the dance floor has always spoken to me of the artful grace that my relationship with God aspires to. In the tradition of ballroom dancing, one partner usually leads and the other follows. This relationship is of the most subtle kind—reminiscent of the gentle guidance of the Holy Spirit in our lives. And the manner in which one leads or follows is again similar to our movements with God.

According to Jennifer Mizendo, an authority on ballroom dancing, dancers communicate with each other primarily through two senses: sight and touch. She writes,

Sight is used by the follower to look for subtle differences or changes in the leader's dance. These differences may include a slight tilt of the head, a change of the level of the hand hold, or even a change of expression in the face of the leader.

We might consider how we too can be similarly attentive to such changes in the countenance of our heavenly Partner. Mizendo comments on the particular characteristics of a good lead.

A leader also uses the sense of sight. He is careful to check for traffic as they are dancing and to know if the follower is ready to be led into a new movement. Through sight, the leader can also see in the follower's eyes and body if she is ready to move on or whether she is satisfied continuing with the same step.

Mizendo's comments about touch are also quite descriptive of the subtle movements that take place in prayer. Consider the following as it compares to how God leads us according to our "sense" of His presence.

Touch is extremely important in the lead/follow relationship. Through maintaining the frame, the lead and the follow must change the degree of pressure in their connection to allow new steps to happen. The actual physical contact between the dancers gives off so much information that it is possible for the follower to dance even with eyes closed.

This type of attentiveness in our relationships is what surely delights God most. Sensitivity to the other makes graceful our spiritual dance.

The leader and the follower must sense the other's entire body through the minimal contact between the hands and the hand at the back. That is all they get. But so much can be learned from this simple contact. Are we going to the right or to the left? Under? Pivot? Slide? Hop?, etc. Through subtle changes of contact, a gentle give and take between the leader and the follower, the dancers know always where they are going next, together in partnership.

As the subtlety of this art develops, so does the gentleness of its directives. If the dancers are fully attentive to one another, a little bit of information goes a long way. As Mizendo puts it, "If the dancers are clear in their contact it can be argued that the lightest touch may be the strongest lead."

The ultimate goal of perfect synchronicity on the dance floor illustrates something of the same unity of wills that Jesus enjoyed with His Father. Mizendo puts it this way,

> Through the lead/follow relationship the dancers create a shared center. No longer are they individuals with separate wills and destiny. They are a unit, separately together, with a shared center between them. When a couple is successful in creating this center they are able to move in the same path of momentum.

Jesus, the "Lord of the Dance," implied as much when He said, "I tell you the truth, the Son can do nothing by himself; he can do only what he sees his Father doing, because whatever the Father does the Son also does." (John 5:19) And Jesus invites us to join Him as He follows the perfect lead of our Father.

57

For everyone who exalts himself will be humbled, and he who humbles himself will be exalted.

Luke 14:1

The basic principle that Jesus presents here is one that is oft repeated in the Bible. The apostle James similarly wrote, "Humble yourselves before the Lord, and he will lift you up" (James 4:10). Peter did as well when he told his followers, "Humble yourselves, therefore, under God's mighty hand, that he may lift you up in due time" (1Pet. 5:6).

We find in Prov. 25:6-7 a teaching that is also similar to Jesus' parable on this topic:

> Do not exalt yourself in the king's presence,
> and do not claim a place among great men;
> it is better for him to say to you, "Come up here,"
> than for him to humiliate you before a nobleman.

The Scriptures agree that when in comes to kingdom values, making yourself small in your own eyes is key to our progress.

Those who are humble don't presume their own status before heaven, but allow God to be the One who defines their worth. They recognize and accept the inevitable truth that, as God judges us, so we are. To humble yourself, then, is to fully trust God's judgment of you. Such trust can only rest in the confidence that His judgments are fair, and in gratitude for the mercy we anticipate.

To justify or exalt yourself in your own eyes is to bypass God. It is to presume a defining knowledge of how you are faring, and to therefore risk the serious likelihood of miscalculation. Jesus warns us that God will surely assert His correctives in our self-assessment.

To humble yourself then is an act of faithful deference. It is being at peace with not knowing precisely how we stand with God. In 1 Cor. 4:3-5, Paul describes his own relationship to this state of deference.

> I care very little if I am judged by you or by any human court; indeed, I do not even judge myself. My conscience is clear, but that does not make me innocent. It is the Lord who judges me.... Therefore judge nothing before the appointed time; wait till the Lord comes. At that time each will receive his praise from God.

We rarely assess ourselves accurately. In the sin of Adam, we presume the office of appraising good and evil for ourselves only to find out, as did our original parents, that we are, at best, poor and inaccurate judges— ones who see shame where no shame is necessary, and pride where no pride is warranted.

In light of such uncertainty, Jesus recommends that it is always better to err on the side of humility. The honour that is then bestowed upon us is doubled in the eyes of God for it is not one that is presumed beforehand. To err on the side of presumption not only robs our Father of His prerogative, it also potentially sets us up for the embarrassment of having our false self publicly exposed. It is better, Jesus says, to approach our Judge with faithful uncertainty than with bold confidence in an error.

Humble yourselves therefore, Jesus tells us, and confidently await God's judgment. This is the supreme act of faith that honours the goodness of the only One whose power and prerogative it is to judge us with righteous judgment, and to reward us according to His good pleasure.

58

For anyone who eats and drinks without recognizing the body of the Lord eats and drinks judgment on themselves.

1 Corinthians 11:29

From the earth, Jesus claimed the fruit of wheat and vine as the ordained place at which to meet Him in remembrance of His sacrifice. Receiving our bread and wine in the spirit of Eucharist tempers us in the direction of the sacrifice it represents. As we prepare to approach our Lord in humble remembrance of this event we have opportunity each week to align the disposition of our hearts to that which is most appropriate for this encounter.

In this prescribed act, we also prepare for the day when we will soon meet our Lord face to face. No longer will bread and wine be the necessary symbols of His sacrifice. Christ's visible wounds themselves will forever prompt our remembrance and our thanksgiving.

We, along with all creation, will one day gather in God's presence before the reality of Christ's historic sacrifice. The prophet Zechariah recorded the words of Jesus saying, "They will look on me, the one they have pierced, and they will mourn" (Zech. 12:10). The apostle John as well saw how the whole world will come to recognize its culpability in necessitating the death of its Saviour. "Every eye will see him, even those who pierced him; and all the peoples of the earth will mourn because of him" (Rev. 1:7). It is in anticipation of this day, and in the soberness of humility, that we who appreciate its significance prepare ourselves.

In Communion, the tempered soul bows in remembrance of Jesus' suffering and sacrifice. As we allow this remembrance to impress us deeply we acknowledge Christ as the remedy for our past and present sins. To do otherwise is to remain conspicuously out of sync with the reality of what is being presented to us. That is why Paul tells his flock that they should be careful to examine themselves before they eat the bread and drink the cup. "For anyone who eats and drinks without recognizing the body of the Lord eats and drinks judgment on themselves" (1 Cor. 11:29). Our mindfulness, or lack thereof, will inevitably judge the disposition of our hearts as either properly recognizing Christ's sacrifice or not.

On the earthly side of its full revelation we have opportunity, as often as we come together, to prepare for this meeting with Love's sacrifice. For Christians, this involves properly discerning the body and blood of Jesus in the bread and wine of Communion. As we gather in remembrance of what the Lord has done for us on the cross and, as we allow the Spirit to lead us in our discernment, we also anticipate the healing of all that is otherwise superficial in us with regards to our salvation.

59

For when I am weak, then I am strong.

2 Corinthians 12:10

One of the great mysteries that Christ demonstrated on the cross was that of the strength and power that exist in what otherwise appears as weakness. Jesus had performed many miracles, had impressed large crowds with his teaching, and shown great personal fortitude in opposing the powers of His day. And yet, nowhere is the paradox of true strength more apparent than in Jesus hanging on the cross.

Christ laid His own strength upon the altar of faith. He put on the garment of weakness in order to more perfectly reveal God's direct hand in our salvation. Jesus' willingness to forego power rested in His full assurance of God's vindication. Paul tells us in Phil. 2:5 that this is the disposition that we too should seek to emulate. We must learn to embrace the mystery of how our own apparent weakness is of much value to God.

In the paradox of spiritual life it is only by embracing the brokenness of our own lives that we become wholly available to God. To deny our weakness—rejecting, in ourselves or in others, what is an essential human condition—is to remain outside the experience of this truth. It is only as we acknowledge and graciously accept ourselves in weakness that we can ever recognize the Lord's compensation.

God's exhortation to the disposition of meekness is one of the foundational expressions of the gospel (Ps. 37.11, Mt. 5:5, 2 Cor. 10:1). It calls us to forego the necessity of strength as our first recourse. Though it challenges our most basic instincts for survival, self-protection, significance and control, we cannot be incarnational Christians without allowing ourselves to become vulnerable. It is this disposition, more than anything else, that provides opportunity for God to reveal His strength.

By accepting our weakness, and that of others, as a sufficient place for God's strength to be revealed we testify most to God's miraculous work of grace. Such grace can only be displayed in those who allow Him opportunity to display His strength in the reality of their weakness.

60

The one who fears God will avoid all extremes.

Ecclesiastes 7:18

Purely and simply, life is exactly what it is. Nothing more, nothing less. But we are often tempted to stretch it into something else, trying to make it into something more than it really is. And this, the Bible teaches, is the very tendency of sin.

Sin is excess. It distorts truth by stretching it out of shape. It takes a good thing and ruins it with greed for more. Gluttony and lust, for instance, are examples of trying to squeeze more out of life than it is actually giving us. So are other sins. Coveting manipulates life beyond what is being offered. Avarice takes our normal need for security and stretches it into a vice. Sloth exaggerates leisure. Anger exaggerates displeasure. Pride exaggerates self-esteem. These are forms of excess that distort life from what it sufficiently is into something more than it should be.

The false nature of sin mars the simple innocence of truth. It exaggerates the self, puffing up our pride. It amplifies our desires, and magnifies the things we lack. It fosters envy, making every other grass look greener. Sin also exaggerates faults, turning a bad thing into something far worse. It sharpens the edges of injury and causes us to obsess on other people's trespasses. It stretches the facts making them much more destructive than need be. Reasonable concerns or cautions turn into paralyzing fears. Self-judgment turns into contempt. A simple weakness becomes a defining identity.

Even good things are exaggerated by sin. Kindness, sacrifice, piety, humility, self-control can all be ruined and made false by excess. Too much kindness becomes pampering. Too much self-control becomes perfectionism. Too much piety becomes self-righteous. Too much humility becomes self-deprecating.

At every turn the enemy of truth stretches us out of shape by distorting the integrity of what actually is. We are lured away from the sure and simple foundation of unadorned reality, and left with the insecurity of its exaggeration.

To be wary of the ways and effects of sin is the first step towards resisting its influence. If we can recognize excess as the obvious trait of sin in our lives it will be much easier to heed the wisdom of Ecclesiastes as it cautions us that, in all our ways, an exaggerated life is something to be avoided.

61

Now devote your heart and soul to seeking the LORD your God. Begin to build the sanctuary of the LORD God, so that you may bring the ark of the covenant of the LORD and the sacred articles belonging to God into the temple that will be built for the Name of the LORD."

1 Chronicles 22:19

In the Old Testament we are often given instructions as to the proper ways to seek and approach God. We are invited to organize ourselves, our environment and our methods, according to what is most conducive to good worship and prayer. Perhaps the idea of such structure might also apply to our often improvised times of prayer.

Prayer naturally has a wandering quality to it. Sometimes it suggests a wonderful sense of adventure as we explore the terrain of our inner life. But wandering can also, at times, feel quite prodigal. That's when the recommendations of Ignatius of Loyola are certainly worth considering.

Ignatius was a methodical man, gifted with skills of administration. In the course of his lifetime, he founded 33 colleges, 15 universities, 176 seminaries, and 74 chapters of the "Society of Jesus," later called the Jesuits. He was a man who appreciated the lasting qualities of a good structure.

We especially recognize Ignatius' regard for good design in his approach to prayer. He understood the value of good preparation, of good goals and of good analysis of our progress. He also taught that, in order to keep growing in our faith, we have to be continually making adjustments in our approach to the spiritual life.

In his *Spiritual Exercises*, Ignatius stressed the importance of preparation for prayer. Assuming that our normal prayer time is in the morning he recommends, for instance, that we begin anticipating this the night before, as we go to bed, and then remain in this focus from the moment we wake up. He writes

> When I awake I will not permit my thoughts to roam at random, but will turn my mind at once to the subject I am about to contemplate in my day.

Before we begin our prayer Ignatius suggests that we take a moment to stand before the place where we will meditate or contemplate and consider that God beholds us here so that we can approach our prayer with more reverence and humility. Reminding ourselves of God's watching presence can also be done at any time if, during our prayer, we feel that we have been wandering.

In the four "weeks" of the *Spiritual Exercises*, Ignatius often asks us to consider what it is that we truly desire—the grace that we seek. It is important to remind ourselves what it is we are seeking and to let that intention guide us throughout the prayer. Is it peace? Gratitude? Joy? Is it a more intimate knowledge of Jesus and his ministry? Is it a greater love for God? Whatever you desire in your prayer, it is good to name it at the onset and to place your request at the door of grace.

Prayer always takes place within the mystery of God's initiative. As we offer ourselves to God it is difficult to know exactly how He will use our time. Does the Lord wish to dialogue with us in our thoughts? Does He wish to reveal Himself through an experience of peace or stillness? Or will He let turmoil instruct us instead? Is He perhaps using this time to show us just how restless and wayward our inner life is? There are many ways that the Lord might use the time we set aside for prayer.

Regardless of what we experience in our prayers, Ignatius recommends that we always end with a review. This is a time to recall the experiences of our prayer and to ask if there is anything in particular that God would want us to note, or to act upon. Is there anything we can learn from today's prayer experience that will help us improve our prayer tomorrow, or our actions today? The review especially applies to the particular grace we have asked for. If, for instance, we originally asked for a greater love for God, is this what our prayer has led us to? If so, we have opportunity to be thankful and to choose to develop this more. If it hasn't, we might consider the reasons why and make the necessary adjustments for tomorrow. Ignatius writes,

> After an exercise is finished, I will consider how I succeeded in the meditation or contemplation. If poorly, I will seek the cause of the failure; and, after I have found it, I will resolve to do better in the future. If I have succeeded I will give thanks to God and will try to follow the same method the next time.

And finally, Ignatius prescribes what he calls the *colloquy*—a friendly, "colloquial" chat with Jesus to end our prayer time. This can be a time to simply thank the Lord for His encouragement, or for expressing our commitment to His purposes, inviting Him to now walk closely with us during our day. In Ignatius' words, we speak to Jesus as "one friend speaks to another, or as a servant speaks to a master, making known our affairs to him, seeking advice or asking a favour."

In all these recommendations we see how the proper administration of time can benefit our prayer. It is through such intentionality that we construct the "sanctuary" in which we hope to meet God.

62

The Word is near you.

Romans 10:8

God is nearer to us than we are to ourselves. This is one of the profound themes that the Orthodox theologian Paul Evdokimov examines in his book, *The Ages of Enlightenment.* He refers to this ontological fact as "the radical proximity of God." God is radically near. He is nearer than we could ever imagine, since even the act of imagining only serves to distance God from us. As Evdokimov writes, "God is closer to us than we are to ourselves. He is before all things, including us, not just in time, but in position." And it is from this "prior" place of interiority that the Lord beckons us.

Evdokimov notes that, "From the depths of His astounding proximity God turns to humans and says, 'I am the Holy One. Come to me.'" It is, however, this very nearness that often makes it difficult for us to recognize God within us. We are unable to see the forest for the trees. As Meister Eckhardt so perceptibly noted, "The eye with which we behold God is same eye with which He beholds us." The reason we don't recognize God's constant gaze is because it *is* so close to us. And it is this over-familiarity that, paradoxically, contributes to our blindness.

The way God moves within us is usually quite natural to us. So much so that it is easy to assume that these movements are our own. When people first recognize God's "voice" within them they are often surprised at how familiar it is. They've always known this voice but they never knew this was God. It takes discernment to be able to distinguish God's movement within us from our own, but it can be done. And the more we recognize the subtle artistry of God, the more we will know what to watch for.

The Lord whispers to us. His communications are as subtle as a breath, nearer than the word on our lips. And in the mystery of God's radical immanence, the more we are able to forego ourselves in favour of what lies behind us, the more we will encounter the very Source of who we are.

63

The LORD longs to be gracious to you; he rises to show you compassion. For the LORD is a God of justice. Blessed are all who wait for him!

Isaiah 30:18

There are times in life when we enjoy a wonderful sense of things being just as they should be. Perhaps we are falling in love, or we've just landed our dream job, or we're off on that long-awaited vacation. Everything seems just right and we'd be quite happy if nothing ever changed. But there are other times when that is certainly not the case. For both identifiable as well as unidentifiable reasons, we often grow restless with life as it is. "What is" somehow doesn't seem enough, and we find ourselves pining for a life other than the one we are presently living.

Some forms of restlessness, of course, are nothing more than the heart's longing for eternity. Others might represent slight adjustments the Lord is making in our relationship to our present situation. But there are other times when such yearnings seem to suggest the birthing of a new, creative vision for our lives. Something is emerging. The Spirit is brooding over the uncreated edges of our lives and, though still formless and void in terms of specific details, we sense that profound changes are imminent.

Such times can either bring hope or frustration, depending on how we relate to them. If we are patient, they can be joyful seasons that anticipate the mystery of what God might have in store for us. But if we are not patient, we will find ourselves instead experiencing turmoil as we strain anxiously to figure out where this is all going. We don't like not knowing what lies ahead and we can easily exhaust our spirits trying to manufacture solutions to our unrest rather than waiting for our spiritual direction to be revealed to us.

Restlessness with "what is" is not always a problem that needs to be solved. Whether we can identify what it is indicating or not we can be confident that there is much creativity going on during these times. Desires are being refined, and our sense of who we are and what we really want in life are being sharpened. Those who can be patient with such stirrings are usually the ones who are most able to recognize the spiritual direction their restlessness is indicating.

Discernment can't be rushed. We often experience the strong desire for change long before we know what it is we are longing for. But we will find creative value in these undefined experiences only if we learn to wait in peace—to gently nurture our longings until they reveal their precise nature to us. In the meantime we can always be confident that our desire for more life than the life we have is a well-founded instinct of the heart.

64

"Teacher, which is the greatest commandment in the Law?"
Jesus replied: " 'Love the Lord your God with all your heart and

with all your soul and with all your mind.' This is the first and greatest commandment. And the second is like it: 'Love your neighbor as yourself.'

Matthew 22:36-39

Jesus certainly made the matter of spiritual direction easy for us. If we are not sure what to do with our lives or with our prayer time we need only return to the most basic teachings of the gospel—the call to love God and to love others.

To desire to grow each day in these two applications of love is to follow God's original intention for our lives. Love is the most complete expression of our humanity. It is what makes us fully alive. Love is who we are. It is not only what we were designed to do, but also who we were meant to be.

To grow in our identity of love then, also represents the healing of our souls. Love for God will free us from the orbit of self-reference that otherwise burdens our lives. And love for our neighbours will melt the very sins of pride, competitiveness, selfishness and envy that keep us isolated from each other.

Love's desire is to be united with the object of its love. This is what our hearts most yearn for—unity with God and with others. We long to see the veil of separation dissolve and our inner lives joined to that which is outside us.

To dwell in love then is to automatically dwell in God. The love we feel for another person is none other than God Himself, present within us for the other person. And the love we feel for God is also God, present within us for Himself. To grow in such love is to be conformed to the very Spirit of God that is active within us. It is to fulfill our role as *imago dei*—images that reflect God's loving nature.

What is the grace that you seek today? I seek O Lord to love you more. I also seek to love others more than I do. I wish to be freed from the many things that prevent me from loving you, and from loving those around me. I desire to be healed of my fears, my insecurity, my pride, my shame so that the blanket they put over my love would be removed. I know that this is also what you most desire for me. Thank you for the faith I have that, each day, your grace works within me towards this beautiful end. Amen.

God is love. Whoever lives in love lives in God, and God in him.
1 John 4:16

65

Therefore let us leave the elementary teachings about Christ and go on to maturity.
Hebrews 6:1

As much as we try to avoid any hint of elitism in matters of faith the fact remains that there are more mature understandings and experiences of faith that we are called to grow in. There truly are milkier and meatier forms of Christianity and the writer of the book of Hebrews calls us to make clear distinctions between what is elemental to our faith and what is the more solid food that leads to maturity. From beginning to full maturity the progression of our faith is something that needs to be clearly taught and understood by all who journey towards God.

Whereas Catholic and Orthodox believers have deep-rooted traditions of holiness, with many persuasions of saints to look to as models of maturity, Protestants are often left with a much more curtailed vision of the spiritual life. After learning the elemental teachings of the faith, our main objective often seems limited to converting others so that, in turn, we can teach these same elemental truths to them. Though there is nothing wrong with this goal in itself, if it becomes the only thrust of our spirituality, it will inevitably represent a thin expression of our faith.

If you were living in the earlier centuries of Christianity and wanted to grow in your faith you would seek out a saint—one who was mature in the wisdom of God and who had grown in prayer to become such an expression of God's proximity that others could learn and model themselves from them. Such men and women were not hard to find though you would likely have to make the effort to seek them beyond the confines of the city or of the institutional church.

Many of these saints became teachers around whom disciples who sought maturity in faith gathered. It was the hunger of the student, more than anything else, that created the many schools of prayer that now anchor our Christian history. As these saints modeled the fruit of spirituality in their lives, a real longing for maturity was encouraged in others by tangible examples of what the spiritual life might actually look like, and by a teaching that came from the first-hand experience of those whose own pilgrimage to God blazed a trail for others to follow.

If we compare the quest for holiness we see in historical Christianity to some of the objectives expressed in many of our present-day models of growth and maturity we find that pep rallies, motivational seminars, conferences and classroom teaching seem to be something of a different order. Have we lost sight of the far-reaching possibilities that exist for maturity in our faith, and of the need to identify the Way of the saints—those who particularly express the fruit of a Christ-united life?

The book of Hebrews encourages us to move beyond the elemental teachings of our faith and to embark on the grand journey that leads to a life more united to God's. This also represents the way forward for the twenty-first century Christian. We too need to be reminded that spiritual growth is not a matter of learning the elemental truths of faith over and over again, but of modeling for one another the bred-in-the-bone reality of what a life devoted to God might actually look like.

Who are the Christians who will once again blaze such trails for us? Who, through their own mature faith, will model for us a sanctity beyond the beginnings of faith? Who will offer themselves to bear such fruit for the sake of others? In every generation the Lord calls forth such men and women. The Holy Spirit whispers in each of our hearts, "Who among you would be a saint?" May those who have ears, hear God's word to them this day.

Who is he who will devote himself to be close to me?

Jeremiah 30:21

ABOUT IMAGO DEI

This is to my Father's glory, that you bear much fruit, showing yourselves to be my disciples.

John 15:8

Jesus bore fruit in individuals, making them His disciples, and then sent them out as ministers in the world—in the marketplace, in their families, among their fellow tradesmen, in their social circles and in their politics. The Lord promised to meet them in a special way whenever they gathered together, but it is clear that His expectations were that the ministry of His Presence and Word would take place as much in the world as among themselves.

As new Imago Dei groups take root in various places we often have to remind ourselves what the fruit of our small ministry is. In a nutshell, the ministry of Imago Dei is not about itself—it's about you, and the fruit you bear as a result of your intimate relationship with Jesus. The ministry of Imago Dei is a means to an end, and not an end in itself. By encouraging your life with Christ, and by creating resources to help you grow in this calling, the hope is that your own God-encouraged ministry will flourish as a result.

It's easy to think of vocation as the prime expression of our lives, as though once we have identified this we need only pour ourselves into it. But spirituality is the real fuel of ministry. Seeking God each day as the wellspring of our lives is the necessary fount for the work we are called to do in this world.

The contemplative pursuit encourages us to find and remain in that place of honest communication with God—the place where our spiritual identities are created, restored and constantly adjusted. The spirit of prayer is the ground from which our active life must be defined and re-defined if it is truly to originate from God. Ultimately our ministry is not what we do, but who we are in the various places God has assigned us.

Community, of course, is essential to our being rooted in the life of the Spirit and we encourage you, wherever you are, to band together with others who share your sincere desire for a more immediate walk with God. Such people are a rare gift to your life—there to remember God's Presence with you. As you allow them to do so, the company of those who know and affirm you will help you be more constant in your spiritual life.

If we can be of any help in encouraging such small communities in your locale please feel free to contact us through our website, www. imagodeicommunity.ca.

Rob Des Cotes
Imago Dei Christian Community

BIBLIOGRAPHY OF
WORKS CITED

Augustine, *Confessions* (New York: Oxford University Press, 1998)

Bounds, E.M., *On Prayer* (Springdale, PA: Whitaker House , 1997)

Brown Taylor, Barbara; *When God Is Silent* (Lanham, Maryland: Rowman & Littlefield Publications, 1998.)

Carretto, Carlo, *In Search of the Beyond* (London: Darton, Longman and Todd, 1975)

de Clairvaux, Bernard, *On Loving God* (Portland, OR: Multnomah Publishing, 1983)

Evan, Nicholas; *The Horse Whisperer* (New York: Dell Publishing Company: 1995)

Evdokimov, Paul. *Ages of the Spiritual Life* (Yonkers, New York: St. Vladimir's Press, 1998)

Guyon, Jeanne, *Experiencing the Depths of Jesus Christ* (Auburn, Maine: Christian Books Publishing House, 1975)

Ignatius of Loyola, *The Spiritual Exercises of St. Ignatius,* translated by Louse J. Puhl, S.J. (Chicago, Ill.: Loyola Press, 1951)

Imbach, Jeff; *The Recovery of Love* (Abbotsford, BC: Fresh Wind Press. 2006)

May, Gerald. *Addiction and Grace* (New York: HarperOne, 1991)

Merton, Thomas, *Thoughts in Solitude* (Boston, Mass.: Shambala Press, 1993)

Mother Teresa, *Total Surrender* (Ann Arbor, Mich: Servant Publications, 1985)

Peterson, Eugene, *Tell It Slant* (Grand Rapids, MI: Wm. B. Eerdmans Publishing, 2008), and *The Contemplative Pastor* (Grand Rapids, MI: Wm. B Eerdmans, 1993).

Picard, Max; *The Word of Silence* (Washington D.C.: Gateway Editions, 1988).

Rohr, Richard, *Everything Belongs* (New York: Crossroad Publishing, 1999).

St. John of the Cross, *The Collected Works of St. John of the Cross* (Washington, DC: ICS Publications, 1991)

Sayings of the Desert Fathers, translated by Benedicta Ward, SLG (Kalamazoo, Mich.: Cistercian Publications 1975)

Steinbeck, John; *The Grapes of Wrath* (New York: Penguin Classics, 1992)

Teresa of Avila, *A Life of Prayer.* Classics of Faith and Devotion. Series, ed. James Houston (Vancouver, B.C.: Regent College Publishing,1998).

Tolkein, J.R R.; *Silmarillion* (New York, NY: Del Rey, 1985)

Tozer, A.W. *The Pursuit of God* (Camp Hill, PA: WingSpread Publishers, 1992)

Van Kaam, Adrian, *Spirituality and the Gentle Life* (Pittsburgh, PA: Epiphany Association, 1994)

SCRIPTURE INDEX